Praise for *Mastering the CPLP*:

"If you want to obtain your CPLP, then you need this book in your hands, not just on your shelf! There is no one I know who has more passion, knowledge, and practical experience in helping people prepare and pass the CPLP than Trish Uhl. This book captures Trish's wisdom and experience and delivers it to you in an easy-to-apply form."

~**BOB PIKE,** CSP, CPAE Speaker Hall of Fame, CPLP Fellow, Author of *Creative Training Techniques*

"*Mastering the CPLP* lives up to its name. Trish Uhl focuses on what one has to *do*, not just what one has to *learn*. The easy-to-navigate concepts and practical tips provide a sound, comprehensive approach to mastering the exam portion of the CPLP requirements. Trish accurately captured the essence of the Kirkpatrick four level model, presenting it in a way that readers will find extremely useful. Trish's supercharged spirit and enthusiasm are woven throughout the book, making it enjoyable to work through."

~**WENDY and JIM KIRKPATRICK,** Author of *Training on Trial*

"When the right person writes the right book for the right purpose in a right way, you get the right results. If you want to pass the CPLP exam, then this is the right book for you."

~**ABDALLAH AL-JURF,** CPLP, T&D Senior Specialist

D1510720

"Trish ROCKS! Learn how to SET your exam prep schedule, MANAGE your emotional intelligence to MINIMIZE your stress, ACCELERATE your learning, and COLLABORATE with others to become the learning LEADER you are meant to be! This book belongs in the hands of all committed or aspiring CPLP candidates!"

~**LOU RUSSELL,** CEO/Project Management Queen, Russell Martin & Associates, Author of *Managing Projects: a Practical Guide for Learning Professionals*

"Trish Uhl is the last word in CPLP prep, taking it far from its American roots to far-flung corners of the globe. This is an excellent guide for those approaching the exam, offering advice for successful brain/knowledge prep as well as many encouraging words and exam survival tips from those who've gone before."

~**JANE BOZARTH,** eLearning Coordinator, State of North Carolina, Author of *Social Media for Trainers: Techniques for Enhancing and Extending Learning*

"A must have, must read, must follow book for every CPLP candidate, *Mastering the CPLP* is a treasure as it is written by Trish Uhl, one of the first CPLP Pilot Pioneers since the beginning of the program in 2005. Since then, Trish has embarked on a mission to empower CPLP candidates globally to succeed by providing training and other resources. This book is a valuable guide for study strategies and techniques. I wish I had such a resource when I took my exam."

~**MAJEDA HAIDAR,** CPLP, Expert IT Education, Central Bank of Kuwait

Mastering the CPLP®: How to Successfully Prepare for—and Pass!—the CPLP Knowledge Exam

Author: Trish Uhl, PMP, CPLP
Cover Design: Helder Magalhaes
Image credit: Kate Wasserman

owl's
ledge LLC

Be Wise

PRINTED IN THE UNITED STATES OF AMERICA
Updated First Edition

The "Certified Professional in Learning & Performance" and "CPLP" are marks of the Association for Talent Development (ATD), formerly the American Society for Training & Development (ASTD).

Mastering the CPLP®:

How to Successfully Prepare for —and Pass!— the CPLP® Knowledge Exam

~ Trish Uhl, PMP, CPLP

Why CPLP?

More and more organizations worldwide are implementing the CPLP internally as a means of:

- Providing a standard approach, consistent framework, and common language for learning and performance

- Ensuring employees' ongoing professional development

- Meeting industry compliance and regulatory requirements

- Modeling best practices required of employees in other professions in the enterprise

- Differentiating themselves from their competition

At this point, you understand the importance of the credential and agree that by earning this designation good things should happen for your career.

I'm sure you have a number of questions.

The following pages answer the most commonly asked questions about several areas, including: the CPLP credential (who is eligible and what's involved in preparing for it?), CPLP Knowledge Exam (what's on it?), and the process of Taking the CPLP

Knowledge Exam (what are the logistics of scheduling and taking the exam?).

~**Lisa Haneberg** I Talent Management/HR/OD Leader I Management and Leadership Author, Speaker, and Consultant

DEDICATION

This book is dedicated to my 2005–2006 CPLP Pilot Pioneer peers who, through laughter, sweat, tears, and many late night calls, blazed new trails in an emerging profession.

And it is in memory of learning leaders:

Dr. Deb Colky, CPLP & Carol Susan DeVaney, CPLP

> *"If we have seen further it is by standing on the shoulders of giants."*

May we aspire to their legacy, and ourselves give back to the learning profession and community in equal measure.

2005-2015 CELEBRATING 10 YEARS of CPLP

2015 Chinese Year of the Ram

PREFACE

Thoughts from Sharon Wingron
That Was Then...

When I transitioned into this career from Industrial Engineering, I knew I had a lot to learn. I did have some experience working with and facilitating quality teams, process improvement initiatives, safety programs, ergonomics, and related training initiatives. But, I needed more. To help with this transition, I had informational interviews with several learning and development professionals, where they consistently told me to join ASTD (at the chapter and society levels), and to explore other related professional societies such as ODN, ISPI, SHRM, ODN, NSA, ICF, IAF, and ASQ.

So, I joined listservs (not to date myself!), attended chapter meetings, and began reading the newsletters and magazines from these organizations. As I immersed myself, I began questioning: What is organization development? How is it different from performance improvement? What is the difference between training and facilitating? When do I do which? Who is ADDIE and why does she matter? Who is Edgar Schein? Peter Drucker? Robert Mager? What's a Thiagi? As I grew in my professional capacity and continued to gain more experience, I got more involved in a few of these professional networks, continuing to learn about the overlaps and distinctions, as well as developing my overall professionalism.

When ASTD undertook the WLP competency study and began formulating the CPLP, I was thrilled to be involved. I had grown quite passionate about this profession and the positive impact we make in the world. As I reviewed the WLP Competency Model, I realized all of those years of seeking, learning, and exploring had paid off. Not only was I familiar with all of the Areas of Expertise to a fairly high degree, I had also built the foundational competencies of networking and partnering, influencing stakeholders, analyzing needs and proposing solutions, thinking strategically, modeling personal development, and more.

This is Now...

Now that the CPLP credential is firmly established, you can learn from the past experiences gained from those who have gone before you. As you prepare for the CPLP Knowledge Exam, you need to educate yourself to be a robust learning and performance professional. In our industry, to be CPLP certified is to be recognized as a multi-disciplinary practitioner capable of leveraging best practices from a variety of disciplines on the learning spectrum, and to apply them to people-focused business solutions.

To be successful (and feel good about what you do!), I encourage you to get involved and learn from ASTD and other industry organizations. Connect with those colleagues—like Trish!—as you prepare and you'll be well-positioned to pass the CPLP Knowledge Exam with flying colors!

~**Sharon Wingron**, CPLP | President, Wings of Success LLC | www.developPEOPLE.com | Past President, St. Louis ASTD Chapter | Past Chair of the ASTD National Advisors for Chapters | First Member of the ASTD Board of Directors to Earn the CPLP Designation

CONTENTS

INTRODUCTION

Accelerated learning to pass the CPLP Knowledge Exam—On Your FIRST Try!

Updated First Edition of Mastering the CPLP Knowledge Exam

by Trish Uhl, PMP, CPLP

Thank you for purchasing the CPLP Knowledge Exam prep book, which is the first book to outline a successful approach for candidates in pursuit of CPLP certification. Our materials have been used all over the world, in the United States and Canada, the Middle East, India, China, Hong Kong, Malaysia, Brazil, the United Kingdom, Europe, and throughout Africa as the premiere approach for CPLP exam prep.

This book follows the same approach we established for passing the exam starting with the CPLP Pilot, when we were the first organization to create the CPLP study prep market in 2005. This approach has been refined over the years, after helping hundreds of successful candidates achieve their dream of CPLP certification.

I am glad that you chose to let us—Owl's Ledge— help you get ready for the exam faster, and without focusing on memorization. After years of experience, we can confirm that the path to *passing* the exam requires more than practicing rote memorization and recitation of materials; exam success requires real education, experience, and exposure—real learning.

We know you are learning professionals, just like we are. That is why this book is full of learning opportunities, not memorization tricks. While other study prep providers force you to memorize, we show you how you can, instead, actually spend the same amount of time learning and pass the exam. I have enjoyed coming up with clever ways for you to get ready for the exam faster and easier. I hope you enjoy this edition!

After working with hundreds of people, I have perfected what our candidates say is the most efficient and shortest process for studying for the exam! As long as you have the right background — education, experience, and exposure—to learning and performance before you start the certification process, candidates should not need to study more than 90 to 120 hours using Owl's Ledge products.

Although you will certainly learn a lot about learning and performance as part of this process, this book is **not** designed to teach you all you need to know about how to design, develop, deliver, or measure and evaluate learning interventions, or about the art and science of improving human performance. You must have a broad range of learning and performance education, experience, and exposure before taking the exam.

In order to get the most out of your efforts and save time studying, this book has been specifically designed to accomplish the following:

– Help you develop your personal Study Plan, not just "throw" you into a bunch of content

– Help you recall past exam success and how you can leverage those experiences and re-familiarize yourself with good study habits to prepare for this exam

– Help you learn, not just memorize

– Focus you on the areas where other candidates struggle

– Help you determine your exam performance gaps

- Provide insider tips about the exam, including tips not found anywhere else

- Help you gain familiarity with different types of exam questions

- Increase your probability of passing the exam on your first try

We know there is a lot of material to cover and that there are many ways to prepare for the CPLP Knowledge Exam. This book presents a time-tested, candidate-approved approach to guide your preparation for taking the CPLP Knowledge Exam, based on your study style and personal preferences, regardless of which study materials and methods you use.

Just to review, the purpose of this book is to focus on a systematic and proven approach to prepare for the CPLP Knowledge Exam. It *IS NOT*:

- A resource to help you to become a better instructional designer, Organization Development (OD) practitioner, performance consultant, facilitator, coach, manager, or overall learning and performance professional

- Designed to educate or expose you to the complex and often dense content contained in the Areas of

Expertise (AOEs) in the Association for Talent Development (ATD) Competency Model

POINTER: Start with a Success

"I started reading from the module I felt I was familiar with the most. This enabled me to get a feeling of the format, content structure, and exercises. I put down a plan by weeks to read the materials, and summarized what I read as I went through the materials. Enough time was left to re-review the materials, which proved to be valuable, as I forgot some of the materials as time passed."

~**Nurit Hattab**, MBA, CPLP | Manager, Knowledge & Learning Center; Global KLC Coordinator, Cisco Video Technologies | First CPLP in Israel

Are You Ready to Take the CPLP Knowledge Exam?

From my experience, most of those who fail the exam do so because they have not had the learning and performance education, experience, or exposure to the broad scope of competencies represented in the ATD Competency Model, and/or because they did not take into account their personal information processing and learning styles. Take both seriously! Real-life experience or just reading a bunch of books in the ATD Learning System is not enough to pass this exam! Books cannot help you answer application level questions like, "You are trying to improve the sales performance of your organization's sales people. They have been through training on the new product line, but are still not closing sales as expected. Which of the following should you do next?" To pass the exam, you need a significant amount of education, experience, and exposure to the integrated competencies outlined in the ATD Competency Model.

Education. Experience. Exposure.

Do you have the skills and knowledge in the learning and performance industry, as represented by the ATD Competency Model, to take this exam? You do not have enough skill and knowledge if you have never done or been involved with the following:

– Used a systematic approach to design and develop training to deliver business results or meet organizational outcomes

– Incorporated adult learning theory, audience demographics, and cultural considerations in the delivery of training

– Prepared and deployed training delivery using a variety of instructional methods, media, learning technologies, and presentation tools and techniques based on learner need and desired business results

– Followed a systematic approach for uncovering the root causes leading to poor performance, selected appropriate interventions to address the underlying issues; developed and deployed an implementation plan, managed change, and used formative and summative evaluation to assess results

– Measured and evaluated learner reaction, compared pre and post assessments to prove learning occurred, evaluated learning transfer to on-the-job behavior, or measured and evaluated business results or organizational outcomes

– Managed a budget, schedule, people, or resources involved in the learning function

– Leveraged principles of systems thinking, theories, and change models to manage and/or drive organizational change

– Determined the differences between information and instruction—and knew when to use which

As you can see, memorizing content is *not* the way to prepare for the CPLP Knowledge Exam. To be successful, you must interact with the material, test it against the framework of your professional experience, and learn how to apply it to the situations represented in the multiple-choice questions on the CPLP Knowledge Exam.

This does not necessarily mean you need years of formal education or a graduate degree in learning and performance to take the CPLP Knowledge Exam. Many current CPLPs started out—as I did—as "Accidental Trainers" without any formal education in learning and performance. Many (myself included) have used the CPLP to quantify and validate their hard-earned, on-the-job professional skills and knowledge.

HOWEVER, if you do not have the education, then you need to have had exposure to the critical competencies in the Areas of Expertise gained through your experience as a learning professional.

ON THE OTHER HAND, for those who have had the education, you still need to have the experience of applying these critical competencies in your practice.

CPLP Knowledge Exam success requires a combination of all three: education, experience, and exposure.

For some, the CPLP certification process presents an opportunity to revisit industry terms and definitions, formal concepts, theories, and models; for others, the study preparation process informs them of professional frameworks and language—perhaps for the first time.

In all cases, whether formally or informally educated, CPLP certification allows you to quantify your skills and knowledge by assessing them against a globally recognized professional standard.

POINTER: For Non-Native English Speakers

"The CPLP Knowledge Exam is in English. If English is not your mother tongue, double the time that you would be spending on an exam material that is written in your native language. Make sure that you 'understand' all of the terminology—in English!— written in your exam preparation materials. On the CPLP exam, you'll face at least one new word in every other question, and that will be tough to understand unless you can figure out the meaning from the context. This needs a good comprehension of the other vocabulary and is found in your preparation materials."

~**Abdallah Aljurf**, CPLP | Training and Development Senior Specialist at National Water Company | First Saudi CPLP, Saudi Arabia

Preparation Approach—Plan, Study, Practice, Prepare

Once you determine that you have the right background and experience to enter the CPLP program, we help you focus on much more than trying to study a bunch of content for exam success. We help our candidates effectively and efficiently prep for the CPLP Knowledge Exam by recommending you follow these steps:

1. Plan

2. Study

3. Practice

4. Prepare

Plan

"Plan your work, work your plan." Straight and simple, you need a personal Study Plan—one that takes into account WHY, WHAT, WHO, WHEN, WHERE, and HOW you plan on preparing for the CPLP Knowledge Exam.

This book walks you step-by-step through my process for helping you put the Why, What, When, Where, and How of your personal Study Plan together.

Study

No way around it, you are going to have to put in the work, which means hours of study time over the course of many months.

The reason being that although CPLP certification is for seasoned learning and performance professionals, studying for an exam about the learning profession:

– is very different than working day-to-day in the profession. Study preparation means familiarizing or re-familiarizing yourself with standard terms and definitions, practicing responding to questions written in the same format and at the same level as found in the Knowledge Exam, and preparing a personalized approach tailored to your preferred study habits.

– requires you to understand that the way for you to be successful in preparing for the CPLP Knowledge Exam is something you have to determine based on your experience, study preferences, and learning style.

Practice

Ultimately, your performance is assessed by the CPLP Knowledge Exam—not your competence as a practitioner at your job, but how well you perform on the exam.

For many of us, it has been a very long time since we took an exam, which means we are out of practice.

Being out of practice, we need to find ways to build up our competence and confidence in test-taking. In this book, you will learn ways to build your test-taking competence and confidence using a variety of tools and techniques.

First, let us take a look at what exactly the CPLP Knowledge Exam is, and what it requires.

CPLP Knowledge Exam Overview

Here are the key facts about the CPLP Knowledge Exam:

– The timed exam consists of 150 computer-based multiple-choice questions from across the Areas of Expertise (AOEs) that must be answered within 150 minutes.

– The questions are designed to assess your ability to know, comprehend, and *apply* the skills and knowledge outlined in the ATD Competency Model.

– The model provides Foundational Competencies as anchors to the integrated professional competencies outlined in the Areas of Expertise (AOEs).

Notice the emphasis on the word *apply*. Do you recall how Bloom's Taxonomy defines application to on-the-job performance? Refer to the image included here for a refresher.

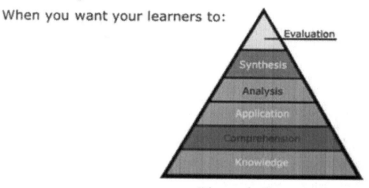

Bloom's Taxonomy

Knowledge Skills Attitudes

When you want your learners to:

Evaluation

Synthesis

Analysis

Application

Comprehension

Knowledge

Bloom's Taxonomy

Let's go a bit deeper with the idea of applying skills and knowledge. The CPLP Knowledge Exam is *not* just a knowledge recall test, nor is it a regurgitation of information. It's a mix of knowledge, comprehension, and application questions which are designed to test your ability to understand and **apply the concepts** covered in the Areas of Expertise (AOEs).

Comprehension and application of knowledge covered in the AOEs is critical for success with the CPLP Knowledge Exam. Understanding the Foundational Competencies from the ATD Competency Model is essential to being successful on the CPLP Knowledge Exam.

Some CPLP candidates mistakenly focus only on the Areas of Expertise in the ATD Competency Model. *Remember — the AOEs are not only meant to be integrated together, they are also meant to be grounded in the Foundational Competencies outlined in the model.* Successful completion of both the CPLP Knowledge Exam and the CPLP Work Product requires candidates to exercise this understanding as part of the certification process.

Ultimately, CPLP candidates are assessed at all levels of Bloom's Taxonomy. The CPLP Knowledge Exam focuses on knowledge, comprehension, and application. The CPLP Work Product focuses on analysis, synthesis, and evaluation.

Prepare

Beyond studying and drilling questions on mock exams for practice, success on the CPLP Knowledge Exam also requires you to be mentally, physically, and emotionally prepared.

Henry Ford once said, "Whether you think you can or can't—you're right."

Mindset is key. I cannot begin to count the number of candidates I have worked with over the years who had to learn to believe in themselves and their work as a necessary first step to clearing barriers to their CPLP certification success.

How are you going to make sure you have the right mindset?

The exam is physically demanding. As a candidate, you will go to an exam center, sit at a monitor (most likely tilted at an awkward angle), while sitting in an uncomfortable chair, answering one multiple-choice question at a time. You may spend a lot of time working at a computer all day, but it's not like this.

How are you going to prepare your body and build your stamina for Exam Day?

Ah, now, emotional intelligence (EQ) has a direct impact on exam success. Some candidates get anxious just thinking about an exam; most candidates experience something frustrating on their way to and/or at the exam center. In either case, being able to manage your own emotional intelligence during the exam could be the difference between success and failure.

How good are you at managing your EQ, especially when you are under stress?

For the remainder of this book, I will show you—in 7 steps—how you can Plan, Study, Practice, and Prepare yourself for mastering the CPLP Knowledge Exam.

7 Steps to CPLP Knowledge Exam Success

The amount of time you need to study, the content used, and your study approach depends on many variables and personal preferences. This book *provides a proven preparation strategy* and planning process for CPLP Knowledge Exam study, as well as a variety of additional tips and techniques used by successful CPLP candidates. The following are the seven (7) steps to prepare for the CPLP Knowledge Exam.

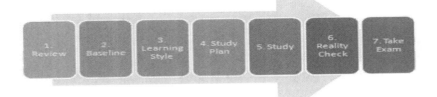

7 Steps:

1. Review the CPLP Program Process and Policies

2. Determine Where You Are/Set Your Baseline

3. Identify Your Learning Preferences & Study Style

4. Create Your Study Plan & Assemble Study Materials

5. Study, Practice, & Prepare

6. Conduct a Reality Check

7. Take the CPLP Knowledge Exam

Included along the way are tips and lessons that I have gathered from my experience working with hundreds of candidates that will help you maximize your preparation efforts. This is *great stuff* that you *won't find anywhere else.*

Here are your first tips!

TIP: Get connected—Join the CPLP Candidate LinkedIn Group! Use this group to connect with other hopeful CPLP candidates and CPLP designees to meet and share information: http://bit.ly/CPLP_LinkedIn

TIP: Start studying and getting up to speed on the credential before you commit to becoming a candidate to save costs and minimize anxiety.

At the end of this book, following these steps, are additional details about the CPLP Knowledge Exam, such as exam day strategies, exam tips, demystifying the exam center, global exam locations, and a bit about special needs.

One final word of wisdom before we get started...

WARNING! The CPLP Knowledge Exam and the manner in which the program is administered by the ATD CI changes frequently! You are responsible for keeping up-to-date with official program policies and procedures for the CPLP certification. Any differences between what is listed here and what is on the ATD Web site should be resolved in favor of the ATD CI Web site. www.td.org/Certification

Step One:
Review the CPLP Program
Policies and Procedures

"Flaming enthusiasm, backed by horse sense and persistence, is the quality that most frequently makes for success." - Dale Carnegie

KEY ACTIONS

–Read the CPLP Certification Handbook

–Review the ATD Competency Model Job Aids

So, are you ready to begin preparation for the CPLP Knowledge Exam? During this first step, you need to get your bearings with an overview of the organization that created it, and know where to find critical information about the CPLP credential and the certification process.

ATD and the ATD Certification Institute (ATD CI)

The Association for Talent Development (ATD) and the ATD Certification Institute (ATD CI) are two separate, but related, entities.

ATD is a professional membership association dedicated to supporting the advancement of the learning and performance profession and the development of learning professionals.

ATD CI is a separate legal entity from ATD, and is responsible for the maintenance and administration of the Certified Professional in Learning and Performance (CPLP) credential. It is also responsible for the definition of and updates to the ATD Competency Model.

All of the ATD CI documentation (the official policies and procedures governing CPLP certification) can be found on the ATD CI Web site (www.td.org/Certification). Official ATD CI documentation for the CPLP Knowledge Exam and the CPLP Work Product submission phases can be found in the CPLP Certification Handbook. The CPLP Certification Handbook is **REQUIRED** reading.

http://bit.ly/CPLPATD

Here are a few key points about the CPLP
Certification Handbook:

– It is available to all visitors to the ATD CI Web site
(www.td.org/Certification). You do not need to be
a registered candidate - or even an ATD member -
to access these materials.

– Proactive candidates also review CPLP Work
Product requirements early in their process —
sometimes before even becoming a candidate — as a
way of setting up themselves up for success. They
do this by ensuring they incorporate CPLP Work
Product requirements into their work so they
OBVIOUSLY DEMONSTRATE their ability to
apply the ATD Competency Model competencies
for their select Area of Expertise (AOE) to their
work and produce work samples at the quality and

caliber demanded by the CPLP certification process.

– The CPLP Certification Handbook is subject to change. Always make sure you visit the ATD CI Web site and download the most current version of the CPLP Certification Handbook BEFORE starting any phase of the CPLP certification process.

TIP: The CPLP Certification Handbook is divided into individual files and appendices on the ATD CI Web site. Each appendix is contained in its own individual Word document or PDF file. This makes it easier for you to select just the appendices you need, when you need them.

http://bit.ly/CPLPHandbook

Your study preparation process truly begins when you download and read the CPLP Certification Handbook. Familiarize yourself with this collection of documents. You will refer to the "Handbook" repeatedly throughout the CPLP certification process. It provides you with information on all of the official policies, procedures, and requirements to meet and complete the CPLP certification process.

For now, focus on just those sections of the CPLP Certification Handbook relevant to the CPLP Knowledge Exam, including:

– **Part 1: Program Overview** Provides a high level, end-to-end overview of the CPLP certification process and policies, including general candidate agreements, Code of Ethics, exam fees, appeals process, and more

– **Part 2: Knowledge Exam** Provides information on the guidelines and administrative process specific to the CPLP Knowledge Exam

– **Content (Body of Knowledge) Outline and ATD Competency Model Job Aids: Action Planning for Individuals** This job aid provides ways for CPLP candidates and the CPLP curious to assess their personal readiness for taking the CPLP Knowledge Exam. Download and review these documents now; you will use them in Step Two.

These sections will not only help you understand what ATD CI expects from CPLP candidates, they will also help you narrow your focus and prioritize the tasks you need to complete first as you start your preparation for the CPLP Knowledge Exam.

International Candidates: In addition to the documents listed above, candidates outside of North America **MUST** also read the "International Candidate Processes" document published on the ATD CI Web site (www.td.org/Certification). This document contains specific details about the exam center locations and the exam scheduling process specific to international candidates.

POINTER:
Network!

"Reach out to people who are CPLP certified, and those who are going through the journey with you!

Once I decided to go for the certification, I joined every possible CPLP networking group I could find at the time. Guess what? 99.9% of the people are willing to reach out and help a total stranger in the process, because that's what we do for a living. We help people succeed!"

~**Ellen Markey** I APAC Customer Services Inc.

Keys to Mastery

In my experience coaching candidates through this process since 2005, failing the CPLP Knowledge

Exam is often due to an incomplete understanding of the program requirements; ignorance of one's information processing preferences and learning styles (covered in Step Three); inadequate education, experience, or exposure before taking the CPLP Knowledge Exam; or a combination of all three. Avoid falling into these traps. Be sure to review and understand the program requirements and the full scope of the CPLP Knowledge Exam. If you are unclear about any aspect of the requirements or scope of the exam—ask! There are many resources at ATD CI, ATD, and your local ATD Chapter (www.td.org/chapters) to help you.

Another key to success in achieving the CPLP credential is to honestly assess your personal readiness for CPLP certification — both for the CPLP Knowledge Exam and the CPLP Work Product. Readiness includes not only the application of the broad subject matter from across all Areas of Expertise, Foundational Competencies, and related work experience, it also requires the right frame of mind to persevere through a demanding process.

Sometimes there are barriers to success. Most often, those barriers are self-imposed. Take some time during this first step to identify any barriers and determine how you can clear them.

Turn the page to get JIMPACTED!

Create Deliberate Awareness to Clear Barriers

"Think about what you do best. Do you inspire others? Do you persevere in the face of adversity? Do you empower others? Whatever things you do best, turn them into consistent actions—make them a way of life and use them as a tool to help you clear barriers to your success.

The first step is to channel your thoughts, actions, energies, and conversations to a positive place. Negative energy fuels negative results.

Then, create a picture in your mind for what this positive future holds for you. See yourself leveraging what you do best into skills or behaviors that you may not have used in some time.

Your mindset drives your behaviors and your results. In other words, thoughts become actions. What you think about, you are about. Get to a place where you focus more on performance and less on excuses.

Finally, listen for and hear all of the praise and recognition that's being directed toward you."

~Jim "Mr. Energy" Smith, Jr. | JIMPACT Enterprises | www.jimpact.com

This brings us to the end of Step One: Review the CPLP Program Process and Policies.

At the end of each chapter in this book, you will find a place to collect your thoughts, review another pointer or two from successful peer CPLP candidates and CPLPs, and, overall, take specific actions to *master* each step.

Use the following checklist to gather your thoughts and to help set your direction.

Also included is a tool contributed by Gerald "SolutionMan" Haman to help you understand your personal goals and motivation for pursuing the CPLP.

Check it out!

Master Step One Now: Review the CPLP Program Process and Policies

This step discussed WHY you want to enter the CPLP certification program and WHY you need to study.

Understanding Program Policies & Procedures

- ☐ Visit the ATD Certification Institute (ATD CI) Web site: www.td.org/Certification

- ☐ Review all CPLP Certification Handbook elements related to the CPLP Knowledge Exam policies, procedures, and scope (Program Overview, Program Policies, and Knowledge Exam Administration, Knowledge Exam - High Level Content Outline, Knowledge Exam - Detailed Content Outline)

- ☐ Record any questions you have based on your review of this information:

- ☐ Record your notes here. How do you meet the Eligibility Requirements? (Check the CPLP Certification Handbook. Candidate Eligibility Requirements were revised in December 2013.)

Organize Information for Your Application

Collect information to complete the application:

□ Background

□ Formal Education

□ Employment History (with references). Be sure to add enough employment experience and references to meet eligibility requirements.

NOTE: You must have your ATD Member/Candidate ID number and password to access the candidate management system. If you do not have an ID number or have misplaced your ID number, contact ATD Member Services at 1.800.628.2783.

CPLP Certification Handbook, Part 2, Appendix F &*Action Planning for Individuals Job Aids*

Download CPLP Certification Handbook, Part 2, Appendix F from the ATD CI Web site. Download the "Action Planning for Individuals" job aid www.td.org/model Read them now. You will work with these documents in Step Two.

□ Appendix F: Knowledge Exam - Detailed Content Outline

□ *Action Planning for Individuals job aid*

Clear Barriers

☐ Channel your thoughts, actions, energies, and conversations into a positive place.

☐ Create a picture of what this positive future holds for you. See yourself leveraging what you do best into skills and accomplishments.

☐ Harness your mindset to drive your behaviors and achieve your results. Thoughts become actions.

Understand Your Personal Goals & Motivation — Coaching Questions Journal

CPLP certification requires you to commit to several months of work to complete the process. You may, as other candidates have, find it helpful to identify your reasons for certification and to document them using the checklist below. These early thoughts can help you keep up your motivation as you progress through the certification process.

– Keep your goal present—why do you want to get certified? *marketability*

– Complete, sign, and post a Commitment Pledge— keep it visible to keep you motivated.

– How will you communicate to others (friends, family, colleagues, superiors) your personal perceived importance in achieving the CPLP certification—and ask them for their support?

KNOW YOURSELF

- ☐ On a scale of 1–10 (1=Poor, 10=Excellent), how would you currently rate your readiness to take the CPLP Knowledge Exam? ①

KNOW GOALS

- ☐ What goals, challenges, or problems do you want to focus on during the CPLP certification process?

- ☐ What do you want to BE as a result of CPLP certification?

- ☐ What do you want to KNOW as a result of CPLP certification?

- ☐ What do you want to FEEL as a result of CPLP certification?

- ☐ What do you want to HAVE as a result of CPLP certification?

- ☐ What do you want to DO as a result of CPLP certification?

KNOW NEEDS

☐ What do you NEED to study?

☐ When do you NEED to study? (How often? What days? For how long?)

☐ Where do you NEED to study?

☐ What inhibits or blocks your ability to study or be successful on a multiple-choice exam? 2 HRS

NOTE: In addition to what you have already identified after reviewing the ATD Competency Model, we provide you with tools you can use to discover which Areas of Expertise you specifically need to study in Step Two.

KNOW BRAINS

☐ What "words" describe the way you think or how your brain works?

☐ How do the above "words" relate to how you study for an exam?

KNOW PROCESSES, MATERIALS, & TECHNIQUES

- ☐ What process(es) do you use to study for an exam?

- ☐ What types of materials do you usually need to study for an exam?

- ☐ What techniques do you use to study for an exam?

NOTE: Beyond what you recall about your past experiences preparing for an exam, we will cover processes, materials, and techniques in greater detail in Steps Three and Four.

KNOW VALUE

- ☐ What is the potential value of your achievement of CPLP certification?

- ☐ What is the potential value of CPLP certification to the organization you support?

move organization forward in their commitment to training — job security

KNOW ACTION

- ☐ What must be your next steps and action plans to start your study preparation?

- ☐ Who must be sold or persuaded to support you in your certification study preparation? · bride supervisor

- ☐ What are potential obstacles or challenges in your certification study preparation? · other income activities

- ☐ What resources must you have to progress? $

- ☐ How must you follow through to guarantee successful results your certification study preparation?

Adapted from Gerald "Solutionman" Haman's Accelerating Innovation & Creativity Workshop SolutionPeople |

www.InnovationTrainingWorkshops.com

34

Step Two:
Determine Where You Are/Set Your Baseline

"Begin with the end in mind." ~Stephen R. Covey

KEY ACTIONS

- Check off items you are familiar with in Appendix F: Knowledge-Exam Content Outline

- Complete the Readiness Assessments by each Area of Expertise and Foundational Competency based on what you checked off (and left unchecked) in Appendix F, using the Action Plan for Individuals job aid as a guide

– Consider what you learned from completing the Readiness Assessments and reviewing Appendix F: Knowledge Exam - Content Outline. What areas require your study focus? How are those areas weighted on the CPLP Knowledge Exam?

– Take the ATD Practice CPLP (pCPLP). Use the pCPLP as another input to determine where to focus your study efforts.

–Record the Areas of Expertise you will need to focus study time on (prioritized by how they are weighted on the exam) as your *baseline* (starting point)

Now that you have an overview of the CPLP credentialing process and policies, it's time to get started planning your personal strategic study approach! Remember the CPLP Certification Handbook documents and Action Planning for Individuals job aid you downloaded in Step One? *Get them out now.*

Many learning professionals find themselves asking questions like these when considering, or after entering the program and becoming a CPLP candidate:

– Am I ready to take the CPLP Knowledge Exam?

– How do I know if I need to improve my knowledge, build my skills, or gain more experience before registering as a CPLP candidate?

These questions are based on understanding where you are with your knowledge, skills, and experience in the learning and performance arena. The best way to determine where you are is to complete the Readiness Assessments, work through the content outline of the body of knowledge covered on the CPLP Knowledge Exam, and take a sample exam. The results of completing these actions become input for building your individual, personalized Study Plan. Let's look at each action.

Readiness Assessments: The self-assessments in the *Action Planning for Individuals job aid* help you evaluate your own expertise, determine your gaps, and select from a variety of learning strategies to bridge the gap for each Area of Expertise (AOE).

These Readiness Assessments are **CRITICAL** inputs to helping you determine your overall state of CPLP readiness and determining where you need to focus your study time on the substantive content assessed on the exam.

Appendix F: Knowledge Exam - Content Outline: This detailed outline provides a listing of the full scope of subject matter on the CPLP Knowledge

Exam. The detailed outline provides granular detail about the knowledge areas and objectives under the ATD Competency Model Areas of Expertise (AOEs) and Foundational Competencies. You should spend A LOT of time with this document throughout your study process! For now, take some time to go through this and check off the items in Appendix F with which you are familiar.

TIP: Placing a checkmark next to items with which you already feel familiar will help to give you a sense of what kind of study commitment you need to make to work through the substantive content and prepare for the exam, based on the items that remain unchecked. There is an additional task to complete to really help you determine where to focus which I'll cover in Step Three, but this first step should begin to give you an idea of how much material you will need to review (overall) to best prepare for the exam.

TIP: After achieving CPLP success and becoming CPLP certified, you will refer to the detailed Content Outline in Appendix F to determine which activities you complete are eligible for recertification credit toward maintaining the CPLP credential.

POINTER: Resist the Temptation to Study What You Know Best

"It's tempting to spend time immersed in content that you love—it's natural to want to stay in your comfort zone. Since time is limited, do an honest assessment of your weak areas and concentrate on those. But remember, certain AOEs are given more emphasis on the exam, so be sure not to overdo studying an AOE that is a small percentage of the total exam."

~**Janet DiVincenzo**, CPLP | University of California, Irvine

TIP: You will discover redundancy in the objectives and subtopics in the CPLP Certification Handbook, Part 2, Appendix F. This is by design, as the competencies in the ATD Competency Model are meant to be integrated together. For example, to function as a professional in learning & performance today - regardless of the Area(s) Expertise you must be competent at performing formative and summative evaluations of your learning programs. Therefore, formative and summative evaluation are critical competencies listed over and over again, throughout the Areas of Expertise in the ATD Competency Model.

POINTER: Strategies to Prepare for the Knowledge Exam

"There is so much information that it's virtually impossible to devote equal time and attention to it all. I started by taking the section/module quiz first, to identify knowledge gaps. This helped me determine how to best use my time by focusing on the content areas where a knowledge gap existed.

Don't get caught up in memorizing names of people, theories, and models .It's more important to understand concepts first, and *then* connect those concepts to people, theories, and models.

Give yourself plenty of time! Don't try cramming all of the material into a short window of time before taking the exam. Treat your exam prep like a project and create a timeline of activities leading up to your examination date."

~**Kristopher J. Newbauer**, CPLP | Rotary International

Spend some quality time with the Readiness Assessments and Appendix F. Your outputs from working with these documents becomes the foundation for your preparation and study approach for the CPLP Knowledge Exam—in other words, they become inputs into your personal Study Plan. Using Appendix F with the Action Planning for

Individuals job aid helps you identify exactly which subject matter you need to focus on as you study.

Next, take the information you gathered from the previous steps and start building your baseline—a starting point you can establish now and use later for comparisons to assess your progress.

In future steps, I will show you how to compare key inputs at the midpoint and end points of your study preparation, against your initial baseline. This will help you to determine how well you are doing with your studying. If necessary, you can revise your preparation methods along the way, if you don't see the progress you hoped for at any point in time.

Consider the information you gathered about your state of readiness in the previous step by using Appendix F and the Action Planning for Individuals job aid. Working with these documents provides input into helping you set your baseline. Knowing your baseline at the start of your study practice can help you monitor your progress later, as you go, so you can make adjustments, as necessary if you're not achieving the performance results you desire at later study stages. *Get those completed documents out now.*

Review your results to determine how much you may already know, and on which areas you need to focus. Specifically, evaluate the following:

– **Action Planning for Individuals:** What areas of strength and weakness did you identify? Did anything there indicate that you may need more time or experience before beginning the CPLP certification process?

– **Appendix F: Knowledge Exam Content Outline:** How many items are unchecked? Which AOEs are they in? Unchecked items represent subject matter you do **not** currently know, comprehend, and/or cannot apply. Use the Content Outline as the basis for determining the subject matter you should focus on in your studies. The unchecked items are where you will focus your efforts. Balance your focus areas against the AOE weighting. You can check later, as you study, to ensure you close the gaps.

TIP: CPLP extraordinaire Star Fisher, member of the leadership team at the Austin ATD Chapter, generously shares the Study Guides she created (based on Appendix C in the old CPLP Candidate Bulletin, the precursor to the CPLP Certification Handbook) when she was a candidate in 2009. Although the content in Star's study guides is outdated, the format of her study guides serve as an excellent model for how to create your own based on Appendix F: http://bit.ly/Star_CPLP

At Owl's Ledge, we provide updated CPLP Knowledge Exam Study Guides (think "Cliff Notes" or "Spark Notes") as part of the Owl's Ledge CPLP Mastery Series

Visit Owl's Ledge CPLP Knowledge Exam study preparation for details: http://bit.ly/OWL_KEprep

POINTER: Take Every Sample Quiz Online That You Can

"Get good at parsing questions and answers. The best way to do this is by taking lots of practice tests. In a spreadsheet, keep track of your score and the date you took each one. Take them repeatedly until you reach a proficiency of 90%."

~**Janet DiVincenzo**, CPLP | University of California, Irvine

TIP: Did you know Areas of Expertise (AOEs) are not weighted equally on the CPLP Knowledge Exam? Some are more heavily weighted than others. For example, Performance Improvement, Instructional Design, and Training Delivery are 16% each, whereas Integrated Talent Management is only 9%. Refer to Appendix F for details. Prioritize your unchecked items in Appendix F and develop your Study Plan accordingly.

Review the number of items you have unchecked in the AOEs with the highest weightings. Unchecked items in an Area of Expertise weighted more heavily on the exam should receive more focus than unchecked items from AOEs with a lower weighting. Many candidates find studying for the exam to be an overwhelming amount of subject matter to study - it is! Appendix F represents the entire body of knowledge that defines the learning & performance profession! Chances are, you're not going to be able to absorb all of this material at the level of application necessary to account for every possible question on the CPLP Knowledge Exam; you need to be strategic about focusing on critical areas first, and the rest as you have time and motivation. This exercise is straightforward: you need to spend more time studying the knowledge area and objectives that remain unchecked and most highly weighted.

Your First CPLP Practice Exam

Remember—CPLP Knowledge Exam success is determined by how well you perform on the CPLP Knowledge Exam, rather than by your competence as a learning professional at your day job.

Performing well on a computerized, multiple choice exam covering a broad body of knowledge is a skill like any other. Skills development (we know - we're learning pros!) require PRACTICE. Make sure you do NOT just consume content; you must drill practice questions to build your COMPETENCE and CONFIDENCE for taking the CPLP Knowledge Exam.

Therefore, it's helpful to establish your baseline early in your study preparation so you can monitor your own performance improvement in building your test taking skills. Monitoring your progress can be done at your midpoint (halfway through your study schedule) against your baseline to see how well your study habits are contributing to improving your exam performance.

If you see little or no improvement at your midpoint (some candidates even see a decrease in performance!), then you have insights & time to make adjustments to what you're studying, how you're studying, and how you practice, rather than continuing to study in a way that does not serve you. Ideally, you want to avoid the rude awakening of finding out on Exam Day that you didn't study or practice in a meaningful, memorable, or motivational way that contributed to your exam success.

How do you become intentional in your study preparation and practice? Take a practice exam to set your testing baseline. The ATD practice CPLP (pCPLP)—offered free to all ATD members as part of their member dues—is perfect for setting your baseline! It's a mock exam made up of retired CPLP Knowledge Exam questions. Take the pCPLP to experience what the official CPLP Knowledge Exam is like.

NOTE: Access to the pCPLP at is free to ATD National members. Use your td.org login credentials to access the pCPLP Web site: http://pcplp.td.org

START NEW EXAM

CPLP Practice Exam - pCPLP™

The purpose of the pCPLP is to help CPLP candidates prepare to take the CPLP multiple choice exam. There are 90 test items. There are no penalties for guessing so it is recommended that you answer all of the items. The pCPLP assessment will take approximately 45 minutes to complete.

1. A workplace learning and performance professional (WLP) opens a CPR certification class with a true story of an employee who became ill at work and was kept alive by a co-worker administering CPR until paramedics arrived. Which adult learning principle is the WLP focusing on?

A ○ Readiness

B ○ Respect

C ○ Autonomy

D ○ Action

☐ Mark this item for later review

Next >   Review All

TIP: The pCPLP exam is delivered using very similar technology and user interface as that used for the official CPLP Knowledge Exam. Although it is not scored the same as the official CPLP Knowledge

Exam, it does allow you to experience the exam questions, exam interface, and get some diagnostics as to your test performance in each AOE.

TIP: Be attentive to how questions are displayed during the pCPLP. Notice how the questions are not labeled by AOE; this is true of the official CPLP Knowledge Exam. You will not be told which AOE a question comes from.

TIP: Keep in mind that although the pCPLP is not scored the same as the official CPLP Knowledge Exam, it does allow you to experience the exam questions, exam interface, and get some diagnostics as to your test performance in each AOE. These are the benefits of a study preparation tool that is, otherwise, limited in scope. Its static question set and easy access make it a good tool for gauging study progress, but not for drilling questions. If you're interested in additional practice questions written at the same level of application and in the same format as the CPLP Knowledge Exam, then checkout my online practice exams and flash cards at: www.CPLPCOACH.com

POINTER: Pareto Algorithm

"I used an algorithm that factored in the following data to determine where I should spend my study time: my pCPLP results taken six months apart—

noting any gains or losses in scores by AOE, the weighted percentages of each Knowledge Exam AOE, and the AOEs where I lacked consistency/confidence or fell below a passing score.

The Owl's Ledge online practice exams provided quick reviews of my high scoring/ low-weighted AOEs where I invested significantly less study time."

~**Linda G. Ackerman**, CPLP | Ackerman & Associates

Example of 2015 CPLP Knowledge Exam Score Report

```
ATD Certification Institute (ATD CI)
Certified Professional in Learning and Performance (CPLP)
Score Report
```

This is to certify that:

```
Name:  Jane Doe
ID #: 222
Examination Date: 03/21/15
Address line 1: 123 Main St
City, State, Zipcode: Chicago, Illinois, 60601
```

was successful in achieving a passing score on the CPLP Knowledge Exam.

The examination covers the following areas:

Diagnostic Indicators

```
Instructional Design: 84%
Training Delivery: 83%
Performance Improvement: 78%
Evaluating Learning Impact: 71%
Managing Learning Programs: 83%
Coaching: 72%
Integrated Talent Management: 72%
Change Management: 76%
Knowledge Management: 71%
```

These test results were achieved on an examination designed to measure key knowledge as defined by the ATD Certification Institute and based on the latest "ASTD Competency Study: The Training & Development Profession Redefined." Use of these test results for any other purpose is not consistent with the design of the examination.

Submission of a successful Work Product is required before certification will be granted. Complete details on the requirements for the Work Product submission and deadlines can be obtained at www.td.org/Certification.

Please contact certification@td.org if you have a change of address.

Once you have your results from the pCPLP, review your high level Diagnostic Indicators (percentage scores) ONLY. Take the pCPLP a second time at your midpoint to reassess your exam performance.

Wait until your midpoint to review the Exam Results—Item Level Feedback. The reason being, the pCPLP exam never changes. If you read too much of the detailed feedback now (at the beginning, during your initial baseline), you are likely to memorize questions and answers, which will skew your performance when you take the pCPLP again. Memorizing answers now will hinder your ability to use the pCPLP as a tool to monitor your progress later.

For now, briefly scan the questions and answers that you got wrong. These incorrect answers give you a better understanding of the AOEs on which you need to focus as you start to study. Compare difficult areas on the pCPLP exam with your checkmarks on Appendix F. Do both tools point to the same content areas or AOEs? If so, that is where you need to focus your study efforts.

Use the Checklist that follows to track your progress for this step.

Master Step Two Now: Determine Where You Are/Set Your Baseline

This step discusses WHAT to study, WHEN, and HOW OFTEN.

☐ Complete the Readiness Assessments in the *Action Planning for Individuals job aid* guide

○ Review your results. Do you have enough experience across all Areas of Expertise to be ready to take the CPLP Knowledge Exam?

○ Are you at a point in your career where you are ready to start the CPLP certification process?

☐ Review the CPLP Certification Handbook, Part 2, Appendix F, Knowledge Exam - Content Outline

Appendix F contains a detailed listing of the knowledge areas and objectives on the exam, as categorized by each Area of Expertise in the ATD Competency Model.

○ Place a checkmark next to each item with which you already feel familiar.

○ Review the document when you are finished.

○ Focus on items that remain unchecked.

○ Prioritize these items against how the AOEs are weighted.

○ Treat unchecked items in an AOE weighted heavily on the CPLP Knowledge Exam as a higher priority than those from a less weighted AOE.

○ Utilize this as your roadmap for keeping track of topics you are familiar with and can apply vs. the areas you do NOT know and/or cannot apply.

○ Use the Content Outline now to set your baseline, but keep a copy of it handy! You will refer to it often throughout your study practice to ensure you are focused on CPLP-related topic areas.

☐ Take the Practice CPLP Exam (pCPLP)

NOTE: The pCPLP is free to all ATD members. You do not need to be registered as a CPLP candidate to take the pCPLP.

○ Visit the pCPLP Web site. http://pcplp.td.org

○ Login using your td.org credentials.

○ Take the pCPLP.

○ Copy and paste the detailed results appear on the screen after you submit your completed assessment into a Word document, and save your report.

○ Other than briefly reviewing which questions you answered incorrectly and noting the percentages you scored in each Area of Expertise, do NOT spend time reviewing the pCPLP detailed feedback. (Otherwise you risk simply learning the correct answers and decrease the effectiveness of using the pCPLP later in your study process to gauge your progress. No worries—you will review the detailed feedback after you take the pCPLP again at your study preparation midpoint.)

Reminder! The CPLP Knowledge Exam consists of knowledge recall, comprehension, *and* application questions (think Bloom's Taxonomy).

Taking the pCPLP exam NOW, at the start of your preparation gives you a baseline measure to help you evaluate your future study progress as well as gives you a better understanding of the areas you need to focus your study on.

The pCPLP consists of questions retired from the official CPLP Knowledge Exam, and is delivered using similar technology as to what you will see the exam center, so the overall experience is helpful in demonstrating to you what the exam is like.

NOTE: The pCPLP is NOT the official CPLP Knowledge Exam. The pCPLP is also not designed or scored the same as the official CPLP Knowledge Exam. Consider your pCPLP score percentages for each Area of Expertise as high-level indicators representing areas where you will want to spend some study time.

CPLP Knowledge Exam Deadlines

☐ Check the Test Schedule on the ATD CI Web site: www.td.org/Certification

☐ Decide on a date.
My target date for taking the CPLP Knowledge Exam is:

☐ Make note of the registration deadline.
CPLP candidate Registration Deadline for your target date is:

My CPLP Knowledge Exam Study Schedule

☐ My date to start studying is: _____

☐ I commit to studying _____ hours per week, for _____ weeks/months

☐ Based on my start date and exam date, my midpoint date is: _____

TIP: How long does it take to prepare for the CPLP Knowledge Exam? On average, CPLP candidates in the United States study approximately 3 to 6 hours per week for 3 months to prepare for the exam. The CPLP Knowledge Exam contains a lot of American English jargon and idioms. Therefore, many candidates outside of the U.S. (especially those with English as a second language) study approximately 3 to 6 hours per week for 4 to 6 months to prepare for the exam, with additional time to practice drilling questions written in American English.

Step Three:
Identify Your Learning
Preferences & Study Style

"There is a difference between interest and commitment. When you're interested in something, you do it only when it's convenient. When you're committed to something, you accept no excuses, only results." ~Ken Blanchard

KEY ACTIONS

- Identify your information processing style, learning preferences, and study style

- Use your preferences and styles to determine how to best study and what materials you need to support your study habits

Preparing for the CPLP Knowledge Exam is more than just reading a bunch of books or other materials to learn or review the content of our profession. Successful preparation is about being self-aware and creating a well thought-out, individual study strategy and plan that will help YOU succeed.

It's ironic—we are learning professionals, yet we often do not take into consideration our own information processing, learning, or study preferences. This step in the process helps you identify or recall, what your learning preferences and study style(s) are so that you can create a plan that works for you. Plan for success. Put together a personal study strategy and plan that honors your preferences and supports your study style.

Be deliberate. Be attentive. Be aware. Setup your personal study strategy to support your certification success!

Roger's Story

Over the years, I have seen many CPLP candidates fail the CPLP Knowledge Exam—not because they were inexperienced or did not put in the study effort, but because they did not interact with the material in the ways they needed in order to truly process and apply the content.

This is Roger's story.

When Roger came to me, he had spent more than 18 months preparing and had two failed attempts at passing the CPLP Knowledge Exam. He was out of money, out of time, and out of ideas about how to improve his performance on the exam.

Roger was isolated in his study practice, because he lived at a great distance from his colleagues. Plus, he did not think that his separation was a problem; he works alone a lot—what's the big deal? He told me that colleagues of his had successfully passed the exam simply by reading the books in the ATD Learning System. He had done the same and had very different results. It seemed that Roger's situation was as I suspected; he assumed that how other candidates prepared for the CPLP Knowledge Exam would automatically work for him.

I asked Roger to take a VARK questionnaire and to email me the results.

Through that process, Roger discovered that he is a strong auditory learner. In working together, we found that in order for Roger to process and internalize information (truly learn), he needs to discuss theories, concepts, and models with people. Together we discovered that Roger benefits from verbally processing information external to himself (he needs to "talk it out") and hearing stories of others' experiences also helps him apply the material to his own experience and cognitive framework. These activities helped Roger make the material "stick." I introduced Roger to other candidates who had similar needs and who were already meeting by phone. Together, they read and discussed the knowledge areas and objectives; conducted teach-backs; and read material out loud. Roger also participated in a synchronous online class to help him better understand some of the terminology, models, theories, and concepts that were new to him.

Three months later, Roger passed the CPLP Knowledge Exam with an impressive score. Understanding his learning preferences and study style were critical factors to Roger's success. Understanding your preferences will be critical to your success, too. You'll see the difference!

It's time to take a look at how you work best in study mode. How do you learn and process information? What are your study preferences? Do you work better in a group or alone? Are you self-motivated or do you need a structured time and place to study?

Information Processing and Learning Preferences

How you process information, the environments in which you learn best, and your study style are all intricately linked. Understanding these very personal aspects is critical to your study preparation and ultimately, your CPLP Knowledge Exam success. Let's begin with learning preference and how you process information. VARK is an acronym which identifies learning styles and how each processes information. The letters stand for: Visual, Auditory, Read/Write, and Kinesthetic. Which of the following is your learning style?

Visual

– Often close their eyes to visualize or remember something

– Benefit from illustrations, mind maps, and presentations that use color

– Are attracted to written or spoken language rich in imagery

POINTER: Mr. Sketch Does Windows

"An accelerated learning technique that has helped me to learn information over the years is to write information and draw mind maps with markers on the glass doors in my house. I would leave these notes up for several days. That way, every time I walked by, I had a chance to see the content. My family even got into it and used those notes to quiz me. Mr. Sketch markers were just the thing—they had a bit of a fragrance, and wiped off easily when I was on to other information to learn!"

~**Lou Russell** | Russell Martin & Associates | www.russellmartin.com

Auditory

– Acquire knowledge by reading aloud

– Remember by verbalizing information to themselves

– Often benefit from discussing information with others or processing information using other verbal formats, such as via teach-backs

POINTER: Auditory Learning Tool

"My favorite tip in preparing for the CPLP Knowledge Exam was utilizing the voice notes recorder on my Blackberry. I would record flashcard answers, concepts, theories—anything I wanted to memorize—and play them back in the car, in the airport, before bed, etc. Great tool for auditory learners!"

~**Jennifer Antos**, CPLP | Gables Residential

Read/Write

– Need to interact with the material by reading it and writing it in another form—notes, mind maps, note cards, flip charts, etc.

POINTER: Do-It-Yourself Flash Cards

"Especially for those of us who are the Read/Write types, just the act of writing something you want to memorize helps to cement it in your brain. Creating flash cards reinforces this concept, and gives you a quick reminder tool that you can pick up and study whenever you have a minute."

~**Marilyn Zwissler**, CPLP | Rockwell Automation

Kinesthetic

– Need to be active—oftentimes in motion—and take frequent breaks

– Remember what was done, but struggle to remember what was said or seen

– Prefer hands-on experience

POINTER: Tie Theory to Practical Experience

"As a kinesthetic learner, I found it useful to take each theory and identify a practical application from my own experience, demonstrating each step in the process. This helped to solidify the process in my mind and ensure understanding."

~**Jacqueline Dutsch**, CPLP | Hilton Worldwide

Multi-Modal

– Uses more than one learning style

– Frequently switches between learning styles to learn

POINTER: Use Multiple Study Tools & Techniques

"As a multi-modal learner, I found that using multiple study tools and methods helped me to absorb all the information as well as learn in a fun and engaging way. The combination of reading and studying the ATD Learning System books, using Owl's Ledge flash cards and the mobile app for practice testing, participating in face-to-face as well as online study groups, using online games and puzzles, and watching the video clips on the ATD Web site—allowed me to successfully learn and remember key theories and concepts as well as apply them to real learning events."

~**Jill Quarles**, CPLP | Hilton Worldwide

Do any or several of these learning styles resonate with you? If you're not sure about your style, or would like to assess your preferences visit:

http://bit.ly/VARK_q

There are many ways to accommodate your learning style as you interact with the material. Be sure to check out the end of this chapter for specific pointers about learning style tips contributed by successful CPLPs.

TIP: Be honest with yourself when identifying your information processing, learning, and study styles. Be sure to address how you will accommodate these styles when developing your study plan.

POINTER: Accelerate Retention by Using What You Know Best—YOURSELF!

"There is so much content to cover for the Knowledge Exam—with multiple AOEs it can be overwhelming! But there's good news! If you learn how YOU learn best, it's so much easier! I'm very RIGHT brained, and an auditory learner. I love making up creative ways to remember things using mnemonics, songs, and even silly sayings. Color coding and pictures helped me remember which AOE topics belonged in when there were subtle differences between two items."

~**Ellen Markey** | APAC Customer Services Inc.

Study Style

Now that you have a sense of learning preference and information processing style, let's look at the element of study style. What is the most effective way for you to study—alone or in groups, or a combination of these? There are many avenues available to you. If you work best in a structured environment or would like to work as part of a group, try these:

Workshops: ATD has more than 100 chapters across the U.S. and 30 Global Networks and partners around the world. Many of these—domestic and international locations—offer CPLP prep workshops to their communities. Check the calendar online or ask your local chapter or Global Network about upcoming CPLP workshops. Check the ATD Web site to find your local chapter or Global Network:

ATD Chapters:

www.td.org/chapters

Contact Wei Wang, Director, International Relations at ATD to learn about ATD Global Networks: international@td.org

Owl's Ledge often partners with ATD chapters and Global Networks to offer CPLP certification preparation workshops—in-classroom and online, as well as public or private. Check www.cplpcoach.com for upcoming events.

Study Groups: Getting together with folks is a GREAT approach for studying and enables learning from each other. It's also good for moral support—not to mention it being more fun than going it alone. A group can help hold you accountable to your study schedule, and keep you motivated for studying when you just don't feel like it. Look for in-person and online study groups provided by your local ATD chapter or Global Network.

TIP: Another great place to find study groups and study partners is on LinkedIn—check the CPLP Candidate Group (and other CPLP related LinkedIn groups) for like-minded individuals: http://bit.ly/CPLP_LinkedIn

So, what have you learned or rediscovered about your learning preferences, information processing style, and study preferences and style? Note these factors about yourself on the checklist that follows. Highlight any of the pointers from other CPLPs that resonate with you and that you may wish to incorporate in your Study Plan. Speaking of the Study Plan, guess what's next… Step Four: Create Your Study Plan & Assemble Study Materials.

Master Step Three Now: Identify Your Learning Preferences & Study Style

This step discusses HOW and WHERE to study, and WHO to study with. This can be especially helpful if it has been a while, as is the case with many candidates, since the last time you prepared for any exam. Therefore, reacquainting yourself with your personal learning style and information processing preferences can be critical components to your certification success! I recommend using the VARK (Visual, Aural, Read/Write, Kinesthetic) Model, but most models will do. The point is to improve your comprehension and decrease your study time by being attentive to your preferences and designing an approach that works best for you.

☐ Identify your learning preferences

○ Take the VARK Questionnaire:

http://bit.ly/VARK_q

○ What are your primary and secondary study styles?

○ How can you accommodate your study styles and learning preferences?

☐ Which learning style strategies work best for you?

- What kind of study location works best for you? (e.g., home, office, library, etc.)

- Study Style—where do you study best?

  o Alone

  o In a group

  o Combination

  o Formal or informal setting

POINTERS:

Visual Learners' Deck

"While the CPLP Knowledge Exam concerns itself solely with the application of learning models, principles, and methodologies, I found it useful to produce a deck of approximately 35 flash cards— each depicting a colorful representation of key learning and performance models ranging from the Herrmann Whole Brain Model and Cog's Ladder to Kepner-Tregoe and Rummler-Brache—all with graphics, thereby satisfying my visual and kinesthetic learning preferences and providing me with a memorable study tool.

The colorful images also facilitated Accelerated Learning. Post-exam, I still love having the deck nearby as a handy reference."

~**Linda G. Ackerman**, CPLP | Ackerman & Associates

Become an Expert in Your Study Group

"An effective study group really helped me learn faster and better—and make new friends. The key for me was that we each accepted responsibility to help each other. Choosing an Area of Expertise in which I served as our group 'expert' helped me prepare that area, and also helped me respect and use what others had prepared."

~**Bruce Mabee**, CPLP | Milestone Partners, LLC

Study with a Friend or a Group

"Study with another candidate or a group of candidates. You can foster your own learning by explaining topics and concepts to others. Explaining material helps you understand it better. Asking questions of each other is also beneficial. The questions you discuss could be similar to questions on the exam!

An example: I studied with a close friend and colleague. We each studied different topics and then asked the other about them. She explained Gagné to me; I explained Kirkpatrick to her. We discussed both theory and practice and found that the Exam was similar to our discussions. We both passed on our first try."

~**John J. McDermott**, CPLP | New Mexico

Step Four:
Create Your Study Plan &
Assemble Study Materials

"Leaders establish the vision for the future and set the strategy for getting there." - John P. Kotter

KEY ACTIONS

–Create a personalized Study Plan

–Identify and secure study materials that support your learning preferences and study style

Up to this point in the process, you have reviewed salient documents in the CPLP Certification Handbook to understand the process, compared what you know with the Appendix F Knowledge Exam - Content Outline, taken the ATD pCPLP for the first time, and identified your learning preferences and study style. All of this preliminary work has produced the input for your plan. You are now ready to put pen to paper and outline your Study Plan. Part of your Study Plan includes identifying study materials that you will use.

Remember Step Two where you checked the items you were familiar with on the Content Outline? *Get it out now.*

POINTER: Make It Manageable!

"Break up the Knowledge Exam content into manageable pieces to study. Create a study schedule to review all of the content prior to the test. Stick to your study schedule!"

~Dr. Kella B. Price, SPHR, CPLP | CEO, HR and Training Consultant | The Price Consulting Group

Create Your Study Plan

Follow these steps to start developing your personal Study Plan:

1. Review the unchecked items you have listed on the Content Outline.

2. Use the Sample Worksheet provided in the *Action Planning for Individuals guide* to record *your findings.*

3. List both your Level of Expertise and Gap for each AOE on the Readiness Assessments.

4. List your learning strategy to address each gap, based on your learning preference and study style. Repeat for each Area of Expertise (AOE).

TIP: Document this information in a Study Guide.

Access 2009 Study Guides from CPLP designee Star Fisher (Austin ASTD): http://bit.ly/Star_CPLP

~ *or* ~

Access updated Study Guides as part of the Owl's Ledge CPLP Mastery Series.

Visit Ow'ls Ledge CPLP Knowledge Exam study preparation for details: http://bit.ly/OWL_KEprep

The CPLP Knowledge Exam requires you to apply subject matter from the integrated Areas of Expertise and Foundational Competencies.

Creating a Study Plan—personal to you—that addresses your learning style, study style, what to study, when to study, and the approach you will use to acquire your selected study materials, is critical to your success on the CPLP Knowledge Exam!

The best way to create your Study Plan is to actually map out your progress over the time you have allocated to study. Get out your calendar, and map your study areas to the weeks between now and your scheduled CPLP Knowledge Exam. If you are part of a team or a group, be sure to include your study partners in the plan.

Don't forget to build milestones into your Study Plan (e.g., at your midpoint). Include activities to help you celebrate reaching significant milestones along the way (e.g., lunch or dinner with a friend). Enjoying a piece of cake also works! (Yay, cake!) The point is to include something you enjoy to reward yourself and build it into your plan. You know what they say about all work and no play...

POINTERS:

You MUST Have a Study Plan

"One of the most important tidbits of advice I received through my personal coaching was that I had, had, HAD to have a study plan—and I had to STICK TO IT! There is no benefit to thinking about planning to study, or even thinking about studying.

The key is to sit down with reality and decide—how much time do I have in a week to study? Hint: 7 days times 24 hours less hours needed to sleep, work, attend to the household—bills, repairs, errands—the kids, pets, plants, etc., equals the number of hours per week available to study. When you do the math, you realize you will NEVER have spare time to study. *You have to make it.*"

~**Diane L. Smith**, CPLP | Everest CS

Study Practice

"I set up a schedule to study each knowledge area (once a week), plus 1 week for review. I took notes and used these as a study guide to review the content at the end of the week. The week before the test, I refocused my studying on content areas that I needed the most review (e.g., address weak knowledge areas and the largest percentage of the test)."

~**Dr. Kella B. Price**, SPHR, CPLP | CEO, HR and Training Consultant | The Price Consulting Group

Study plans come in all shapes and sizes. Sometimes it's easier to build something when you have an example or two to consider. Here is one example of a high-level study approach used by successful CPLP candidates. It illustrates how a team of two can establish individual plans and work together to hold each other accountable.

Team Approach Example

– **Start a Study Group:** Reach out to people to find those who are available and willing to meet. In this case, it ended up being two people. The study partners met every Saturday morning for 3 hours.

– **Determine Baselines:** Each study partner took the pCPLP exam right away. They used their scores, along with the AOEs' percentage on the exam to determine where to spend the largest part of their preparation time.

– **Create Individual Study Plans:** Not everyone has the same knowledge gaps or learning styles. Each study partner created her own study plan and shared it with the other. This way, each had her own plan but together they devised ways to work as a team, share materials, and take ownership for content areas to cover.

– **Assemble Materials:** The study team used the ATD Learning System as one of their resources, but not the only resource for content.

– **Study/Prepare:** They attended the Owl's Ledge CPLP Mastery Series Knowledge Exam Prep Course (it's a self-study and 90 minutes of online facilitation per week).

– **Divide and Conquer:** The study partners divided the AOE topics between them and chose an AOE each week. Some harder or more complex AOEs took two weeks.

Many Friday nights were spent preparing for the study group. They researched the topics assigned to them (one half of the AOE topics in Appendix F: Knowledge Exam - Content Outline) and made notes in order to teach this content to their partner.

Saturday mornings, they switched off teaching each other the key concepts for the AOE. For any unclear topics, they would refer to their resources and figure it out together.

(Renie McClay, CPLP and Melissa Pagonis, CPLP study partners)

POINTER: Reach Out to a 'Study Buddy' or Two

"My study buddy and I happened to be in the same geographic location, but meeting with someone virtually will have the same impact for holding each other accountable. After we each registered for the exam, we worked backwards from that date to create a study schedule and treated it like a second job. Being committed to each other and our process helped us to successfully pass the exam on the first try!"

~Cristina Masucci, CPLP | HSBC

When developing your Study Plan, be specific about the plans and strategies you will use each step of the way. Map out your overall study strategy (e.g., How will you approach your study preparation? What is your timeframe for taking the exam? How much time per week can you devote to studying?), determine how you will consume the content, and come up with an approach to follow in the final "push" before taking the CPLP Knowledge Exam.

TIP: Use a variety of preparation methods and materials! Variety adds interest, stimulates deeper learning, and supports different learning styles.

POINTER: Local Study Group

"As a member of the ATD Las Vegas chapter, options were given on how CPLP candidates could learn and study material. The chapter president even set up online events and partnered with other chapters to maximize exposure and support.

I got the best results through face-to-face study group sessions. The most critical part of my success was the interaction. We assigned leads for each of our study sessions. This helped me reinforce my learning through prep for delivering to the group. We treated the sessions like regular training workshops and incorporated activities to help us retain what we were learning.

When I took the exam, I felt confident that I had what I needed to pass. I admit taking a deep breath when I hit 'send' to submit, but I have to say that I wasn't surprised to see the word 'pass,' because my study group prepared me so well for my desired outcome!"

~**Kim Leahy**, CPLP | Nevada State Bank

Identify Study Materials

In addition to mapping out your time and the process you will follow in your Study Plan, you need to identify where you will find the material to help you study or learn the topics, terminology, and concepts covered on the CPLP Knowledge Exam. There are many sources of material available—some are complete sets of content, others are specific to topics or Areas of Expertise found in the ATD Competency Model.

Question: "I am planning on taking the CPLP soon and was wondering if I need to purchase the entire ATD Learning System from ATD or if there might be a more cost effective but still comprehensive way to learn?"

What a great question. There are a number of options available, and the ATD Learning System is one of them. The Learning System is a multi-volume set covering most (but not all) of the content found in the ATD Competency Model. More information about this learning system can be found on the ATD Web site. Whether or not you should invest in this depends on what you need to study and your personal best practices for studying. If you like to read and would like to have summary material in one central location, this may be a good option for you. Another option to consider is to acquire the original texts on which the ATD Learning System is based. Oftentimes, many CPLP candidates possess or have access to these resources. Visit www.cplpcoach.com/public/extras for a detailed list of resources.

TIP: *The ATD Learning System is particularly good for folks or companies who don't have a lot of material in their libraries—and are looking for a central repository of substantive information for the certification and beyond—and/or folks who have others in their departments who might use the Learning System at a later date. Sharing the Learning System can help to offset the cost.*

TIP: *Make sure you use your local Chapter Incentive Program (ChIP) code when placing any order with ATD—whether paying membership dues, purchasing the ATD Learning System, registering for an education workshop, or applying to become a CPLP candidate. ChIP helps local chapters with funding so they can provide improved support to local CPLP candidates and learning professionals.*

If you are considering purchasing the ATD Learning System, think about becoming a member of ATD National. Membership provides benefits such as access to the pCPLP and member-only material hosted on the ATD Web site, TD magazine, and discounts on other products/services. Plus, ATD members get a discount on the CPLP registration fees. You will spend the money either way—why not get more for your money and save money at the same time?

TIP: If you use the ATD Learning System, keep the following in mind:

— *The Learning System periodically goes thru updates. Be sure to check to see if you have the most up-to-date material. The updates are available for free online at*: *www.td*.org

— *Do not rely solely on the questions contained at the end of each chapter. Most Learning System questions do not reflect the same style or the same level of the questions on the official CPLP Knowledge Exam. Use the material, but look for additional and alternative methods to practice answering exam questions.*

POINTER: Think outside the box!

"If you use it, don't merely memorize content from the ATD Learning System. Dissect it, draw it on paper (or with a PDA or tablet drawing app), say it out loud, tell someone else about it (hopefully in an ATD study group). Discuss with colleagues how the knowledge can be applied on the job as a learning professional. Share drawbacks and caveats. Identify enablers. Think outside the 'learning system' box!"

~**Bob Zimel**, CPLP | Learning Executive

Aside from the ATD Learning System, there are many other sources to help you find content or to augment what you already have. Here are some thoughts on finding materials to help you with the CPLP Knowledge Exam:

Keep the following types of materials in mind when completing your assessment and identifying materials to help you close any knowledge gaps.

- **ATD:** The ATD Web site (www.td.org) contains quite a bit of study preparation materials included in ATD membership. For example, members have access to the ATD pCPLP (practice exam), and the ATD Career Navigator (an online assessment against the ATD Competency Model).

- **Quizlet:** Savvy CPLP candidates all over the world are using social media platforms like Quizlet (www.quizlet.com) to create and share flash cards and other study aids. We are too! Owl's Ledge uses the Quizlet platform to provide its self-study and workshop candidates with 400+ mobile and printable flash cards!

- **Books and "Short Content":** There are a number of books by publishers such as Pfeiffer which contain detailed subject matter covered by the Knowledge Exam. There are also shorter resources available ("short content") that cover certain topics on the Knowledge Exam.

– **Infolines** are ATD publications containing fewer than 20 pages, covering practical information for immediate proficiency in a wide variety of learning and performance topics. Find them at the ATD Web site.

– **Online Resources:** Using Google to find resources can be great (all hail Google!). However, Google is *not* the only search engine out there. Additional search engines exist and can be used to find online resources. For example, try www.clusty.com to get different results than Google and www.kartoo.com for results with a visual twist.

– **Local Library:** Many materials are found in local libraries. Be sure to include local community college libraries too!

– **Local ATD Chapter or Global Network:** See if it offers services like ATD Learning System loans, study groups, or Special Interest Groups (SIGs). There are 100+ local ATD chapters in the United States and 10+ Global Networks worldwide. You can find your local chapter — or global network — by checking www.td.org/chapters.

– **Owl's Ledge:** We offer a variety of ways to prepare for the CPLP Knowledge Exam—from self-study, to facilitated online and in-classroom training.

Review Owl's Ledge CPLP Knowledge Exam study preparation options: www.bit.ly/OWL_KEprep

POINTER: Use These for Study Help

– **Books:** The authors and publishers you choose can make a huge difference—are the materials easy to learn from, engaging, and do they provide activities to put your new knowledge to work?

– **Instructor-Led Training (ILT) Workshops:** Besides having an amazingly knowledgeable and engaging facilitator, workshops also put you in contact with other people who want to learn, and who can share their learning experiences with you.

- **CPLP Coach:** Owl's Ledge offers a variety of tools, techniques, and resources to help with all phases of preparation for the CPLP credential. Some resources include:

  - Flash Cards

  - Online Practice Exams

  - Mobile Apps

  - Games

  - Puzzles

  - Study Guides

  - Online Facilitated Workshops

  - In-Classroom Facilitated Workshops

- **Online Resources:** Besides knowledge content, there are social Web sites where you can connect with like-minded candidates who need and can give study guidance. Sometimes we can learn more and better when we teach others.

- **Study Groups:** Most people think of a study group as a face-to-face encounter with other candidates. These are everywhere, and sometimes nowhere to be found. However; all of the three resources listed above are 'groups' to study from and with.

"Do not limit your study group to a table if you can't find people to sit with. The world of CPLP is full of very willing teachers and students. You can connect to any number of them on LinkedIn, Twitter, Facebook, and Flickr. They're a fun group, a close group, and they love to share!"

~**Diane L. Smith**, CPLP | Everest CS

Creating your Study Plan is a big step, and it provides the framework for the weeks you have allocated to prepare for the CPLP Knowledge Exam. It's great to have some samples to look at and some tips and pointers to consider from those who have been successful. After evaluating all of the information, YOU need to identify how to go about studying in a way that supports YOUR learning style.

The bottom line: make a commitment to yourself and to this process. Put a plan in place that works for you, and execute against that plan. Set aside time to concentrate on the task at hand—no distractions!

POINTER: My Experience

"My favorite tip for preparing for the CPLP knowledge exam is to break down the AOE modules per period of time. I began the journey by doing the pCPLP to assess my overall knowledge in all areas, and then I planned on studying one module per week. By the end each week, I would take the quizzes and the pCPLP for that specific module, and if my score was below 90%, I dedicated more time to review that module.

As a multi-modal learner, I used reading aloud, highlighting, making notes, and placing reminder papers in all of my learning systems books. But besides reading and studying the ATD Learning System books, I also used flash cards, quizzes, CDs, the LinkedIn CPLP discussion board, plus I also benefited from discussing the new knowledge with other learning professionals. This helped me to engrain the material and recall the most important concepts and theories."

~**Tatiany Maranhão Melecchi**, CPLP | ASTD St. Louis Board of Directors

Now that we have covered the elements of creating a Study Plan, it's time to just do it! Use the checklist on the following pages to help you get started. Once you have gone through the checklist items, use the activity which follows to "Start with the End in Mind." This activity, contributed by Jim and Wendy Kirkpatrick, is based on Don Kirkpatrick's the Four Levels of Learning. It's a GREAT reality check—a way to help you frame why you are pursuing the CPLP, and just what you need to consider.

Master Step Four Now: Create Your Study Plan & Assemble Study Materials

- ☐ Elements of your personal Study Plan—designing your plan—include:

  - ○ Making note of unchecked items from Appendix F: Knowledge Exam - Content Outline

  - ○ Recording expertise and knowledge gaps in the Readiness Assessment worksheets or Study Guides

  - ○ Recording your study styles and learning preferences

- ☐ Gather study materials and learning assets

  - ○ Pfeiffer "Short Content"

  - ○ Infolines (ATD Publications)

  - ○ Learning and Performance-Related Books (Pfeiffer)

  - ○ ATD Learning System

  - ○ Online Resources (flash cards, games, puzzles, study guides, practice exams, etc.)

  - ○ Mobile Resources (flash cards, practice exams, etc.)

- ○ Public Library (many libraries have wonderful periodical databases that often have full-text articles—and access from home is possible!)

- ○ Classes/Workshops

- ○ Study Group

- ☐ Create your Study Plan

The End is the Beginning

Before you dive right in to earn an industry-recognized credential, take a few moments to map your high level plan using the four levels in reverse:

The Kirkpatrick Model

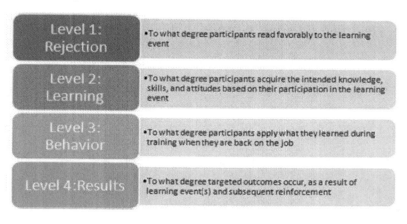

Level 1: Rejection	•To what degree participants read favorably to the learning event
Level 2: Learning	•To what degree participants acquire the intended knowledge, skills, and attitudes based on their participation in the learning event
Level 3: Behavior	•To what degree participants apply what they learned during training when they are back on the job
Level 4: Results	•To what degree targeted outcomes occur, as a result of learning event(s) and subsequent reinforcement

Level 4 Results

What is the highest level result you wish to accomplish by earning your CPLP? Examples include:

– Earn a promotion or pay increase

– Remain viable as a training professional

– Accomplish a personal goal of continued education and improvement

Earning the CPLP is a lengthy and rigorous process. Some days you may be tempted to delay it or give up. Post your highest level goal in a place where you will see it every day to remind you why the effort is worth it.

Level 3 Behavior

Use the steps outlined in this book to define exactly what you need to do to prepare for and earn your CPLP. Add these steps to your calendar and stick to them!

Identify at least one "required driver" for each step: processes and systems that will reinforce, monitor, encourage, and reward you for performing the required steps or behaviors. Some examples are:

– Peer study groups (reinforcement)

– Reward for yourself when you complete a step in the preparation process (reward)

– Peer review appointments: you and a buddy check in with each other on set days and review your progress (monitoring)

– Find someone who has already earned their CPLP, or a supportive boss or executive. Let them know your plans and the result you wish to accomplish. Pick someone who will provide positive messages and support when you need it (encouragement)

Identify at least one "required driver" for each step that will reinforce, monitor, encourage, and reward you for performing the required steps or behaviors:

1. Review the CPLP Program Process & Policies

☐ Driver:

2. Determine Where You Are

☐ Driver:

3. Create Your Study Plan and Assemble Study Materials

☐ Driver:

4. Study, Practice, and Prepare

☐ Driver:

5. Conduct a Reality Check

    □ Driver:

Level 2: Learning

As part of your Level 3 plan, you have identified areas where you need to learn more to pass the exam and prepare your work sample:

    □ Break these things down into chunks and make a learning schedule

    □ Use peers and the available CPLP prep resources to test your knowledge

Level 1: Reaction

Give yourself a pulse check:

    □ Ask: Does your plan pass the "get real" test?

    □ Ensure you have set up a plan with realistic goals and deadlines, and built in checkpoints for yourself

If you plan your CPLP process using the four levels in reverse, you will have a strong plan to begin your journey!

~Jim and Wendy Kirkpatrick | Kirkpatrick Partners
www.kirkpatrickpartners.com

POINTERS:

Study Buddy—Accountability Buddy

"What I found successful in preparing for the CPLP certification was to have a study buddy who was also my accountability buddy. This helped me immensely with both the Knowledge Exam and the Work Product. Even if you have to work with someone virtually, it is great having someone on your side who knows exactly what you are going through at each phase to help you succeed."

~**Larry Straining**, CPLP | Larry's Training, LLC

Study Tips

"1. Never study alone. Find a study buddy to study with you. Not only does this provide an opportunity to validate your knowledge as you study, but it also provides an accountability partner to ensure you are both on target for your exam date.

2. For rote memorization, I often use word association or word pictures to help me remember the information. Having a more visual association helps lock the information in my mind better."

~**Leonard Cochran**, CPLP | Hilton Worldwide

Develop New Knowledge

"This is so true! And it is one of the unheralded results of going through the CPLP certification process. The 'knowledge' we gain in our college/university classes is expanded and used as a result of the connections made in this experience."

~**Marilyn Zwissler**, CPLP | Rockwell Automation

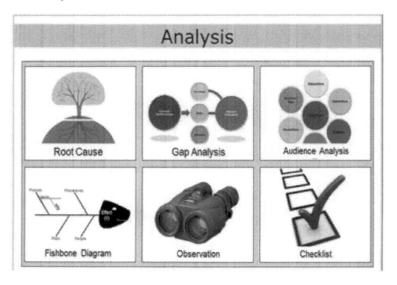

Use CPLP Fellow Bob Pike's "window-paning" technique to draw six (6) window panes that display six (6) critical pieces of information – like the Analysis example I have listed here. We – humans – find information much easier to retain by being able to recall the pictures (which give us the concept)

than if we had simply created a traditional (e.g. bulleted) list.

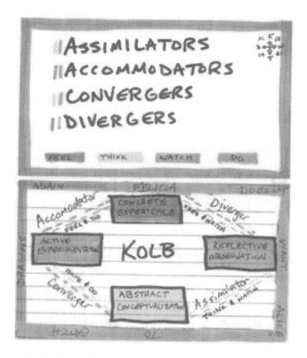

Cory Archibald's flash cards are an EXCELLENT example of implementing multiple accelerated learning techniques – the use of colorful, visually stimulating flash cards, which Cory created herself.

Step Five:
Study, Practice, & Prepare

"This may be a perfect opportunity to use common sense!"
- Bob Pike

KEY ACTIONS

–Interact with the material in multiple ways to support information processing and learning.

In the previous step, you created your individual Study Plan that addresses your preferences and styles for learning. In this step, we will look at specific methods to give your study time meaning—ways to make it "stick."

Adults—we're a funny bunch! Research shows that we learn more effectively when the learning has relevance to us and to our situation. Research shows that the same holds true for studying.

Studying works better when you can connect the material to something else. These relationships don't have to be earth shattering, important, or complex — and quite often can be silly, illogical, and fun! There are a number of ways to give material meaning, including mnemonics, techniques to memorize steps, methods to get the gist of the material and other ideas to help you connect with the content.

There are numerous study methods to use. The key is to find out what works best for you. Here are just a few study methods to get you started.

Concentration: Focus on the task at hand and eliminate distraction by establishing a routine, studying in a designated "study space," knowing your objectives for that study session, and identifying your incentives. Vary your study activities and topics, take breaks, and reward yourself!

Memorization: Use memorization techniques to identify strategies that will help you make the information "stick."

Acronym: Use a combination of letters that represent the first letter of each word. For example, think of the acronym **ADDIE** to help you remember the five Phases (**A**nalysis, **D**esign, **D**evelopment, **I**mplementation, and **E**valuation) that represent the process traditionally used by instructional designers and training developers to build effective training and performance support tools.

Acrostic: Create a made-up sentence or poem where the first letter of each word presents a clue (e.g., **E**very **G**ood **B**oy **D**oes **F**ine to represent the five keys—EGBDF—on the treble clef on a piano keyboard). An acrostic is a kind of mnemonic.

Mind Maps are diagrams used to visually outline information. Start by outlining a specific Area of Expertise based on the information in CPLP Certification Handbook, Part 2, The Knowledge Exam, High Level Content Outline. Put the main theme (e.g., Instructional Design) in the middle, then surround it with a visual representation for each knowledge area. Add the individual objectives to each knowledge area. As you study, continue to add visually to your Mind Map. Research shows that Mind Maps enhance comprehension, information organization, and capacity for reflection.

Mind Mapping is an excellent way to start interacting with the exhaustive information listed in Appendix F. It provides candidates with a visual note-taking technique that helps them to start "chunking" and processing the full scope of any one Area of Expertise.

Mnemonics are "tricks" used to memorize something. A mnemonic usually consists of a word, phrase, rhyme, or sing-song about something easy that helps us to remember something more complex. Here is an example.

Many of us in the United States grew up with "Please Excuse My Dear Aunt Sally."

This mnemonic is used to help children remember the algebraic mathematical order of operations — Parentheses, Exponents, Multiplication, Division, Addition, then Subtraction. In this example, each letter of the mnemonic (e.g., "P" for Parentheses) is given a corresponding word with the same letter (e.g., "P" for Please) in a silly sing-song sentence. If you can remember the sentence (and most do) you can remember the order.

POINTERS:

Cheering on Mnemonics

"Anyone who has ever met me knows I am not very sequential. I was afraid I would not be able to recite back Gagne's 9 steps in order. So I came up with a cheer for innovative instruction. "GO R&D UP FAR!" It didn't relate to instructional design or make any sense but I know Gagne's steps — in order! — to this day!

G = gain attention

O = objectives

R = recall prior learning

D = deliver new content

U = (enhance) understanding

P = practice

F = feedback

A = assess

R = resources

One last thing... When you think of something that helps YOU remember, share the wealth! It just might help others on their journey too!"

~**Ellen Markey** | APAC Customer Services Inc.

Use Your Own Words

"It's critical to use your own words — don't just copy a phrase from the book. Research shows that we remember our own (active) connections better than ones given to us (passive); that our own hierarchies are generally better than the best prefabricated hierarchies."

~**Marilyn Zwissler**, CPLP | Rockwell Automation

Another study technique is the *SQ3R Method* (Robinson, 1970). This is a 5-step process for achieving active elaboration: **S**urvey, **Q**uestion, **R**ead, **R**ecite, and **R**eview.

Using this method is especially effective if you're studying with the ATD Learning System. We will use reading as an example.

Here are the 5 steps to achieve elaboration with written material — ANY written material:

1. Survey (1 minute): Before beginning to read, look through the whole chapter, "Infoline," or article. Pay attention to the headings and subheadings. Our brains love to latch on to hierarchical structures! Try not to actually read the material yet;

just see if you can identify 3 to 6 major ideas in the material.

2. **Question** (usually less than 30 seconds): Ask yourself what the material is about: What is the question it is trying to answer? You can also ask: what question do I have that this material might help answer? Repeat this process with each subsection of the material. Turn each heading into a question.

3. **Read:** Now you're ready to begin reading the material. Read one section at a time, looking for the answer to the question proposed by the heading. This is active reading. Active reading means that you are *not* just scanning the material. Active reading requires concentration, so make sure you're somewhere with a block of time that you can devote to quiet concentration.

4. **Recite/Write** (about a minute): Say to yourself, in your head or out loud—which is an especially fun exercise on the commuter train—or write down (you're allowed to doodle in the margins of the material) a key phrase that sums up the major point of the section and answers the question.

It's critical to use your own words — don't just copy a phrase from the book. Research shows that we remember our own (active) connections better than ones given to us (passive); that our own hierarchies are generally better than the best prefabricated hierarchies.

5. **Review** (less than 5 minutes): After repeating Steps 2–4 for each section, you have a list of key phrases that provides a makeshift outline for the material. Test yourself by covering up the key phrases and seeing if you can recall them.

Do this right after you finish reading the material. If you can't recall one of your major points, that's a section you need to reread.

TIP: SQ3R can be a very effective study method for breaking down the material referenced in the Content (Body of Knowledge) Outline upon which the CPLP Knowledge Exam is based.

TIP: Study Early, Study Often; Take Breaks. Studies show that most people require natural, mini breaks (e.g., stare out the window, let the mind wander, etc.) every 25 minutes or so. In addition, after 45 minutes of intense concentration, most people need to physically move around a bit.

Incorporate these natural tendencies into your study practices by studying in intervals of 25 to 40 minutes, followed by breaks of 5 to 10 minutes. This approach is more effective than trying to "cram" for hours on end. Have you been there, done that, and it didn't go well at all?

POINTER: Taking Breaks in the 150-Minute CPLP Knowledge Exam

"Maintaining mental and physical fitness during the 150-minute exam is crucial. Taking small breaks serve biological needs as well as allowing for stretching. I purposely took a 5 to 7 minute break after the first hour in the exam, even though my progress was a bit behind schedule. After this refreshing time, I was rejuvenated, highly engaged, and concentrated. Finally, I completed all questions and passed the CPLP Knowledge Exam with the first try!"

~**Peter Yip, CPLP** | President | ASTD Global Network Hong Kong

We often take coloring breaks to relax, give our brains a break, and de-stress during Owl's Ledge CPLP online facilitated sessions. The owl connect-the-dots you see here also serves as beautiful visual icon of something we—that specific cohort of candidates—created together. It makes all of us smile to see it!

POINTER: Reinforce Your Study—Write Your Own Multiple-choice Test Questions

"The CPLP Knowledge Exam consists exclusively of multiple-choice questions with many focusing on testing for on-the-job application and not merely recall of information. You might be thinking, 'what's the difference?' Consider these two examples:

Q: What does the letter 'I' in the ADDIE model stand for?

A: Implementation

Q: You sent a detailed design document to a group of SMEs to solicit their feedback and have incorporated a number of their suggestions into the program design. What element in the ADDIE model does this represent?

A: Design

The first item measures recall and the second measures on-the-job application

So when creating your practice test questions, be sure to use multiple-choice questions that focus on on-the-job application and not just recall.

A technique to help you write application focused multiple-choice test questions is to think about real life job situations as you read through your CPLP prep materials and come across various concepts, models and theories.

Draw from your experience

Think about how you could apply these concepts, models or theories in real live job situations:

1. **Draft the question:** Select one of the situations and write the stem (the question or problem) in 1 to 3 sentences.

2. **Write the correct answer:** Next, write the correct answer.

3. **Write the distractors:** Then, identify 3 plausible distractors by thinking about things someone might say or do who thought they knew the concept, model, or theory, but really didn't understand. These make great distractors."

~**Ken Phillips**, PhD., CPLP | Phillips Associates | www.phillipsassociates.com

Have you ever used teach-backs as a study method? I have found this to be a very useful tool. To explain this method briefly, assign a topic to prepare to each person in a study group. Have each person "teach back" that topic to the group. Teach-backs are an excellent way to learn and reinforce the material. There are a number of interesting variations on this basic method. Here is a teach-back technique with a Thiagi twist!

A Twist on Teach Backs—TAKE A GUESS

Activity time: 3 minutes

At the beginning of your teach-back, announce your topic and tell your study partners to pair up (triads are okay too, so that no one is left out). With their partners, create a list of 3 to 6 important facts about the topic that they think you will cover in your presentation. While you talk, they circle any items on their list that you mention. They can also add facts to their lists as directed by you.

When you finish your teach back, ask for a few volunteers to tell the group what they feel is the most important fact on their lists.

This technique keeps your study partners alert, interested, and motivated to listen. You've focused their minds on what they know and on what you want them to know.

~**Sharon Bowman,** Reprinted from PLAY FOR PERFORMANCE, Copyright ©2002 by Workshops by Thiagi, Inc.

POINTER: Teach to Learn

"The best way to learn something is to teach it to others.

When you finish studying one module, summarize it and teach it to your workplace colleagues, friends, or anybody who could:

a. understand what you say.

b. be willing to listen to you.

c. ask you questions that would challenge your understanding and encourage you to get deeper knowledge about the subject that you are teaching."

~**Abdallah Aljurf**, CPLP | First Saudi CPLP, Saudi Arabia

Use a study approach, or better yet, use multiple approaches to really learn the subject matter in a way that helps you to process, internalize, and own it! Studying for the CPLP Knowledge Exam is a long and sometimes overwhelming task. Some days will go well, and others not so much. The following pointer by Maureen Orey provides some great keys to keeping your resilience up during the Knowledge Exam preparation. For more details about these 5 keys to resilience, see the checklist that follows this chapter.

POINTER: Rev Up Your Resilience

"Preparing for the CPLP can be a daunting task! Learning the full body of knowledge for any industry takes dedication, commitment, and a willingness to stay the course. The pressure of work and home obligations on top of the weeks, days, and hours of study and preparation requires you to maintain a certain level of resilience.

Here are five (5) keys to keeping your resilience in high gear:

1. Stay Connected to Your Network

2. Develop New Knowledge

3. Maintain Your Knowledge and Skills

4. Stay Healthy

5. Keep Your Eye on the Goal"

~**Maureen Orey**, CPLP | Workplace Learning and Performance Group | www.wlpgroup.com (See pages 119-121 for details)

Now you're ready for action! Decide on which study method(s) you will use to review the material. The main point here is to *prepare a personal study strategy*—one that supports your best study practices. This is critical to your success.

Master Step Five Now: Study, Practice, & Prepare

□ Identify study methods that work for you:

- Concentration, Memorization, Acronym

- Mind Maps

- Creating Mnemonics

- SQ3R

- Practice Writing Your Own Multiple-choice Questions

- Study Groups

- Games

- Flash Cards

- Puzzles

- Instructor-Led Activities

- Mobile Apps

- Audio

- Summarization Techniques

- Using Teach-Backs

- Reviews (Live Sessions/Books)

○ Study Guides/Spark Notes/Cliff Notes

○ Crossword Puzzles

○ Window Panes

○ ATD Career Navigator

○ Quizlet

○ Other:

POINTERS:

Flash Cards

"For each Module, complete 3" x 5" flash cards with questions on one side; include the module name and page number of the content. On the other side, write the answer. Put the cards into separate envelopes for each module. You should have one envelope for each AOE with module-specific cards by the time we all get together to study, quiz each other, discuss, etc."

~Janet DiVincenzo, CPLP | University of California, Irvine

Don't Cram for the Exam

"I find it best to not cram at the last minute before a test or exam. Cramming gets me confused because I don't know the topic well. It builds up unnecessary stress and anxiety at the last minute. I study in advance of the exam date and review the day before. The day of the exam, I try and rest in the assurance that I have prepared as well as I can and by being calm and rested, I trust that my mind will be able to recall what I need when I need to know it."

~**Leonard Cochran**, CPLP | Hilton Worldwide

Study Smart

"I crammed all my study into less than three months before the exam, I studied alone, I worked without a study plan… I was so pressured and stressed out. I did my first pCPLP exam the night before the exam. I took the exam without having much sleep the night before and was red-eyed.

This was one of the most horrible experiences in my life. Although I passed on my first attempt in December 2009, I wish I had done it differently.

My advice—study smart and not only hard. Use the Mastering the CPLP Knowledge Exam book—it is a treasure. I wish I'd had such a resource back then."

~**Majeda Haidar**, CPLP | Expert IT Education | Central Bank of Kuwait

Tapping into Your Resilience

"Here are details around the five (5) keys that can help you be resilient while on your journey to becoming a Certified Professional in Learning & Performance:

1. Stay Connected to Your Network

Don't do this alone! Whether it be a virtual team, your family, or simply your colleagues at work, invite others to assist you with your studies. One CPLP candidate I knew purchased flash cards and every time someone was in her office, she asked them to pull a card and quiz her! Another candidate kept the flash cards in her car and had her children quiz her as they went to and from school. In addition to your personal network, tap into your local ATD chapter, Facebook, LinkedIn.

2. Develop New Knowledge

Of course it goes without saying that you will develop new knowledge as you prepare for the exam; and completing a self-assessment about your strengths and weaknesses with the multiple AOEs is essential. One main benefit of study prep is that new learning occurs, so first, focus your studies on learning the AOEs that are unfamiliar to you. Oliver Wendell Holmes said, 'A mind once expanded by a new idea, never regains its original dimension.' Your professional growth in the field of learning and performance as a result of the pursuit of your studies can never be taken away. Regardless of the outcome of the certification process, the depth of your knowledge in this field will be forever deeper.

3. Maintain Your Knowledge and Skills

Certainly you would not be going through this process if you were not an experienced learning and performance professional, so don't underestimate the existing knowledge and skill you have in this industry. As a result of their studies, many candidates have realized that they know and practice a particular technique or process in training design or delivery; but they did not realize the original source of the practice or methodology, or did not know the attributed industry terminology. One of the wonderful results of the study and preparation for the CPLP is that you start to feel more connected to the industry as a whole.

4. Stay Healthy

The stress of test prep along with test anxiety for some can make this process a bit nerve-wracking. Be sure to take care of YOU as you study, practice and prepare for the certification. Eat well, sleep well, and exercise. The importance of balancing all of the aspects of your life should not be under-estimated.

You will perform better on the exam and in every part of your life if you can find the right balance.

5. Keep Your Eye on the Goal

As with any goal, there may be obstacles you encounter along the way. It's essential to keep your focus—not only on the goal of completing the CPLP—but also to keep in mind the career and professional benefits that come as a result of your achievement. You will have industry recognition as a Certified Professional in Learning and Performance professional; you will gain credibility as a learning and performance professional; and you may very well find new or enhanced career opportunities!"

~Maureen Orey, CPLP | Workplace Learning and Performance Group | www.wlpgroup.com

Step Six:
Conduct a Reality Check

"Feedback is the breakfast of champions." - Ken Blanchard

KEY ACTIONS

– Measure your progress

– Don't freak out because your study time is nearly done

Question:*"I've been following my study plan and devouring the content. The Knowledge Exam is approaching. How do I check my progress?"*

Good question! The best way to see how you are doing is to take the pCPLP to check your results! This practice exam is located on the ATD Web site at: www.td.org/Certification. You can take the pCPLP for free.

I suggest you take the pCPLP three (3) times during your study practice:

1. First, to set a baseline at the beginning of the process. (This was recommended as an action item in Step 3: Set Your Baseline).

2. Second, at the midpoint to check progress. (Schedule your midpoint at the halfway point in your study preparation timeline.)

3. Third, within a week of sitting the CPLP Knowledge Exam—to, again, see progress, practice getting into the "rhythm" of answering multiple-choice questions, and to get an emotional boost before taking the official exam.

Compare your results along the way each time you take the pCPLP exam. How are you doing? Are there areas in which you consistently struggle? Are these the same areas that are unchecked on your Content Outline? If so, go back to those AOEs and drill a bit more. Or, are these areas that you had checked off? Maybe it's time for a refresher on some of those AOEs you had not focused on.

POINTER: Use Practice Tests—But Beware

"I used practice exam questions based on the materials I used. The practice questions were similar in content and format to the Knowledge Exam questions. One warning about this: the wording on the CPLP Knowledge Exam questions can sometimes be similar to those used in your study preparation materials. Don't confuse the two! Read the CPLP Knowledge Exam questions carefully, so you are answering the specific question before you, rather than answering from your memory of another question. The answer that you knew from the practice question may not be quite right on the exam."

~**Marilyn Zwissler**, CPLP | Rockwell Automation

TIP: In the final two weeks of preparation, use these steps to see where you are:

1. Re-review each AOE section and notes from your reading/studying.

2. Drill questions.

3. Take the pCPLP.

4. Review the "The End is the Beginning" activity from Jim and Wendy Kirkpatrick at the end of Step 5. How are you doing? Recall what you wish to accomplish by earning your CPLP.

POINTER: Take a Practice Test!

"One to two weeks before your test date, take a practice test to see where you should focus your last-minute review time. Taking a 'dry run' helps you to know where to focus your time and boosts your confidence when you see how well prepared you really are!"

~**Kris Kern Stark**, CPLP I Kohl's Department Stores

At this point in the process, I typically get some frantic calls and emails from candidates. Study time is running out and the Knowledge Exam date is quickly approaching. They may have taken the pCPLP exam and there are still a few areas that are still causing them problems. They are beginning to have real concerns about passing the exam. Here is the type of question candidates pose:

"I've been reading the same thing over and over and it's not sinking in. Help! What should I do?"

We've all been there. Here is a short process that will help you to actively read and absorb the content. This is a great exercise to use when studying solo, in pairs, or even when studying as a group! Give it a try!

1. Read one or two paragraphs of material on a specific subject.

2. Write a 20-word (or less) summary about the gist of what you've read.

3. Read, watch, draw, doodle, mind map, or listen to an additional one or two "paragraphs" of related material. This technique reinforces learning and understanding by making it more memorable through layering the content in your memory using different media.

4. Incorporate the additional information into a new 20-word summary.

5. Depending on the material, you might be able to add the gist of another paragraph or two to your summary without going over the 20-word count.

The outcome of this exercise produces not only a concise summary of the material that's helpful during your review process, but it also forces you to analyze and synthesize the information.

By analyzing and synthesizing the material (e.g., breaking it down and rearranging it into a summary of 20 words or less), you are learning the material at a deeper level than that required by the CPLP Knowledge Exam. (Think Bloom's Taxonomy!)

By doing this you will have moved past Knowledge, Comprehension, and Application, on into Analysis and Synthesis. And, as an extra benefit, through this process you actually learn something — concepts that you might even apply to your work. Imagine that — two benefits for one effort!

This ends the section about the steps for successful CPLP Knowledge Exam preparation. The next section of the book covers all kinds of information about the actual CPLP Knowledge Exam — the physical location, tips before the exam day, tips for taking the exam, what success looks like, locations of testing centers, special needs, and more!

Master Step Six Now: Conduct a Reality Check

☐ Monitor your progress using the pCPLP:

ATD members can re-take the pCPLP as many times as they like, without paying any additional fees. However, the questions on the pCPLP do not change. Therefore, it is important to be strategic in when you take the pCPLP so you can maximize its use.

I recommend taking the pCPLP three (3) times:

1. At the start of your study preparation (baseline)

2. In the middle of your study preparation (midpoint)

3. Within a week of taking the official CPLP Knowledge Exam (endpoint)

   ○ Retake the pCPLP

   ○ Compare your results to the last time you took the pCPLP (baseline, midpoint)

   ○ Have you made progress?

☐ Refer back to the Kirkpatricks' tool—"Begin with the Ending" (referenced at the end of Step 5). Look back at the steps to see how you are doing on the path of what you wish to accomplish by earning your CPLP.

- ☐ Last Two Weeks Review:

  - ○ Revisit the CPLP Certification Handbook, Part 2, Appendix F, Knowledge Exam - Content Outline; look for gaps in your understanding of topics under each Area of Expertise.

  - ○ DRILL! Practice answering multiple-choice questions.

  - ○ Retake pCPLP (endpoint)

  - ○ Review your own notes

- ☐ Describe how you will CELEBRATE success! Rewards and Recognition are important— consider how you will reward yourself and recognize all of your hard work preparing for the CPLP Knowledge Exam, regardless of your outcome.

Step Seven:
Taking the CPLP Knowledge Exam

"I believe life has a turning point—a point at which we either grasp our opportunity to experience AWESOME or we let it slip away." - Jim "Mr. Energy" Smith, Jr.

KEY ACTIONS

- Understand the facts about the Exam and the Exam location
- Get organized ahead of time
- Review pointers to do your best on the Exam

Now that we've covered a proven process that you can use for preparing for the CPLP Knowledge Exam, it's time to talk about the exam itself. I'll take the mystery out of the exam and give you some tips for preparing for Exam Day. Let's start by reviewing the specifics of the CPLP Knowledge Exam.

Knowledge Exam Key Facts:

– It consists of 150 multiple-choice questions which are derived from subject matter taken from across the Areas of Expertise (AOEs) as outlined in the ATD Competency Model.

– Many questions are situational (application level), requiring you to have firsthand knowledge of the same or similar experience for you to respond correctly to the question.

– There are approximately 25 to 30 questions on the exam that do not count toward your exam score. As is common practice for many professional and academic exams, the CPLP Knowledge Exam contains experimental questions (otherwise known as "items"). These questions do *not* count toward candidates' scores and are used by ATD CI to test item validity for possible inclusion in future versions of the CPLP Knowledge Exam.

– On average, candidates need to answer 65% of the CPLP test items correctly to pass.

– The CPLP Knowledge Exam is written in English and is presented in English, regardless of where you take the exam.

– The exam time is 2 hours and 30 minutes. Yes, that's 150 minutes for 150 questions—the math is easy—one question per minute. Obviously, there's no time for dawdling during the exam! Questions are displayed one at a time on the computer screen. The screen does not provide information about which AOE(s) the question belongs to.

TIP: The experimental questions are not labeled in any way—there's no way to tell which questions are experimental and which are scored. You are better off answering every question as if it counted toward your score. Guessing is better than leaving a question unanswered. If you are unsure about a question, click the checkmark to 'Mark for Review' and come back to it later. Just be mindful of your time.

POINTER: Finding the BEST Answer Can Be Tricky!

"Many questions did not resemble the mock exam questions from the ATD pCPLP or Owl's Ledge practice exams. They were different, and covered many areas that I did not come across before. Plus, it seemed that 2 out of 4 multiple-choice answers were similar."

~Faridah "Ibu" Hanim | Learning Specialist | Organizational Development & Change

Management, PETRONAS Leadership Centre |
Malaysia

No matter how well you study, there will always be
a few questions that you won't understand let alone
know what the correct answer is. On questions like
these, make a choice, and return to them later. Don't
waste time dwelling on them! AND, make sure you
answer ALL questions. There's no penalty for
guessing—and guesses (even random ones) could
work in your favor!

POINTER: Read the Questions and Answers Carefully—Look for the BEST Answer!

"I tried to read the questions REALLY carefully—if
you miss a very important word, it changes your
whole answer. Look for the KEYWORD—don't just
read the question once. Sometimes I read questions
two or three times in order to fully comprehend
them before answering. I also found that I needed to
reread and really consider all four possible answers
before responding. Make sure you compare the four
answers until you find the BEST answer!"

~**Shirley Ng** | Coach Infinity Company | Hong
Kong

The computer allows you to tag questions you want
to 'Mark for Review.' Candidates often use this
technique to mark questions they're unsure of, and

to return to them after completing (but before submitting!) final answers for the CPLP Knowledge Exam. This feature allows candidates to tag questions they have a little (or a lot of) trouble with, and quickly move on to questions they can more readily answer. Once you have completed all the questions, return to those you've marked and spend more time with them.

TIP: Trusting your first instinct and going with your initial answer on a multiple-choice test is a myth. Research shows that changing answers generally results in a higher test score. After additional reflection, changing an answer may result in a better choice.

TIP: You can practice using the 'Mark for Review' feature during your study preparation when taking the pCPLP exam!

POINTER: Don't Get Easily Discouraged!

"When I took my CPLP Knowledge Exam I was well into questions 13, 14, 15, etc., before I answered my first question. But I knew I need not get discouraged if I read a question I didn't immediately know the answer to. Don't lose hope. It's not unusual for an exam taker to read several of the first questions and realize—for whatever reason—they can't answer them. Don't sweat it—mark that question for review and move on. Keep doing so until you find a question you can answer. They will be there. Once you answer one, more will follow, and your confidence and recall will build. You will be able to go back to the ones you marked for review and attempt an answer. Information in other questions with help trigger your recall. Don't be hard on yourself, just keep going."

~**Coline Son Lee** | Everest CS

Multiple-Choice Exam Strategies

As we've mentioned, the Knowledge Exam is about application, not just recall. Slow down and look for the BEST answer, *not* just the first correct answer. Here are a few strategies to help you read each choice and choose the best answer for each question:

- Speed reading or skimming the question can be a disadvantage because you can miss words that could change the meaning of the question. Always read the question completely, at least twice, before answering. That way you will be sure you are responding to what is actually being asked.

- Don't give in to the temptation to click the first correct answer you see. There may be several correct answers. Remember you need to select the BEST answer of those provided!

– Read the answers in a non-traditional or non-linear fashion. For example in the U.S. we are taught to read from left to right, and from top down (A to D). Re-training yourself to read the multiple-choice answers in a different order than you normally would forces your brain to slow down and really take in what you're reading. This gives you a better chance of identifying the BEST answer, rather than stopping at the first correct answer.

TIP: Many CPLP candidates have mentioned that several questions seemed to have more than one correct answer. Often, most, if not all, of the answers are reasonable responses to the question. (That's good test design—just ask CPLP and measurement & evaluation guru Ken Phillips!) However, there is always one "best" response, as determined by ATD CI—the group who developed and maintains the CPLP Knowledge Exam. This is also why drilling questions based on ATD materials is key: it helps you get into the minds of the exam creators so you can more easily and effectively respond to questions on exam day!

Tips for Taking the Exam

– **Take Your Time:** Although there are a lot of questions (150), take your time to read each one thoughtfully to be sure you know what it is asking.

– **Don't Dwell on Questions:** Answer each as best as you can, or guess. (There's no penalty for guessing.)

– **If Unsure, Mark It:** After answering a question that you're unsure of, mark it so you can easily circle back to it. Be sure you answer it first, in case you don't have time to go back to it!

– **When You're Finished:** Clicking the Submit button at the end of Knowledge Exam is the longest 60 seconds of your life. Everyone experiences this feeling. Breathe!

You'll know your pass or fail status *before* you leave the testing center.

POINTER: You Don't Need to Ace the Exam!

"If you're a perfectionist like me, you'll want to get a perfect score. Although that may be a worthy and ambitious goal, remind yourself that you only need to PASS the exam. No one will see your score (unless you show them). So whether someone scores 65%

(the minimum passing score) or 99%, you've both passed.

Reminding yourself of this will help reduce performance anxiety. All you need be concerned with is how the areas of expertise are weighted so you can place emphasis on performing better on the areas weighted more heavily and thereby increasing your overall chances for success.

Realize that you don't know everything; you will miss some questions. Accept it. Get over it. Move on. Don't waste time and mental energy on a question you simply don't know the answer to. Spend that time on the ones you do know the answers to, and increase your chances of success."

~Coline Son Lee, CPLP | Everest CS

TIP: As part of your preparations to sit for the CPLP Knowledge Exam, make plans to do something rewarding afterwards. You've earned it! Do something that works for you (e.g., have some cake or chocolate, get a pedicure or massage, have a glass of wine, a pint of beer)!

Yay cake!

Demystifying the Exam Center

The exam centers provide standardized, proctored testing environments and adhere to a series of rules when administering the CPLP Knowledge Exam. These procedures include monitoring of exam candidates by staff observation or video/audio monitoring. They do this to make sure that all candidates earn their results under comparable conditions.

Other rules state that friends or relatives who accompany you to the test center will not be permitted to wait in the test center or contact you while you are taking the exam. Also, if you arrive 15 minutes *after* your scheduled appointment, you may be required to forfeit your appointment, reregister for testing, and pay an additional examination fee.

Except where permitted by special accommodation under the Americans with Disabilities Act (ADA), *none* of the following are permitted in the testing room:

- papers

- books

- food and drink

- calculators

– smoking materials

– access to purses, wallets, briefcases, backpacks, bags, cell phones, pagers, palm pilots, MP3 players, watches

Global Exam Locations

Candidates located outside of the U.S. or Canada are referred to as "international candidates." International candidates should refer to the ATD CI Web site for instructions on how to schedule testing for exam centers.

Questions about global exam centers should be directed to ATD CI: certification@td.org

Candidates located in the U.S. and Canada can schedule their exam by using the online scheduling system.

Special Accommodation Arrangements

ATD CI follows all Americans with Disabilities Act (ADA) guidelines and requirements. If you require special testing arrangements, be sure to submit a written request at the time you apply to the CPLP program. Your request must contain information from a qualified medical professional with details about your special accommodation needs.

Examples of circumstances where special accommodations may be necessary include: attention deficit disorder (ADD); physical challenges such as pregnancy, incontinence, or severe allergies; visual impairments, or physical impairments. Special accommodations may include additional time to take the exam, screen magnification, reader services, and separate room availability. More detailed information about special accommodations is available in the CPLP Certification Handbook, Part 2, Appendix F.

Before Exam Day

Successful candidates start preparing themselves for the big event several days to a week before the day of the exam. Consider the following tips to help you prepare for the big day and reduce your stress:

– **Drive to your selected exam facility before the day of the exam.** This way you'll know where it is and how to get to get there. Otherwise, you may find yourself driving like a maniac on exam day and worrying about being lost and late.

– **Go inside and check out the facility.** This is especially good for folks who are sensitive to a test environment.

– **Practice sitting in an uncomfortable chair in front of your computer monitor for a couple of hours at a time.** Get to know your physical, emotional, and mental reactions. How often do you need a break? Record this information and use it to develop your strategy.

– **The test is 150 minutes long—how often will you need a break?** What kind of break? Will you just need to close your eyes or will you need to get up and walk around? Just keep in mind—the clock does not stop running.

- **Don't stay up all night the night before and cram!** Studies show that last minute cramming and lack of sleep are two of the worst things you can do before exam day.

- **Get organized.** Organize the things you will take with you the night before the exam to avoid rushing on exam day.

Bottom line: Do what you can to minimize your exam day anxiety.

POINTER: Do a Dry Run

"To minimize test-day nerves, visit the testing center in advance. You don't have to go in to the testing center; just familiarize yourself with the location and where to park, etc. You don't want to be stressing out about these things on the day of the test."

~Janet DiVincenzo, CPLP | University of California, Irvine

Exam Day

The big day has arrived! You are probably feeling many emotions—nervousness, anxiety, anticipation, and the feeling of wanting to get it over with. Use these tips as a final run through before you leave for the Knowledge Exam.

– **ID:** Bring the proper identification. You are required to bring TWO (2) forms of ID. If you are not sure what identification is acceptable, ask someone at ATD CI.

– **Authorization:** Bring a printed copy of your candidate authorization email. This email contains your Test Taker Authorization Code. You will *not* be able to launch your exam at the test center if you do *not* have your code.

– **Be Comfortable:** Wear something that you will be comfortable in for several hours. Make sure nothing is restrictive or binding. Wear shoes and clothes that make you feel comfortable and confident.

– **Don't Run on Empty:** Eat a little something beforehand so you don't get hungry while taking the CPLP Knowledge Exam. Nutritionists recommend pre-test meals should consist of high-fiber carbohydrates—leafy greens (spinach, romaine lettuce) plus some lean protein (dark-meat chicken or turkey with the skin removed; pork tenderloin; seafood like tuna, salmon, herring; egg whites). It's difficult to focus when your stomach is growling or you have a headache because you are hungry. (Also—avoid high-fat, over-size meals the night before!)

- **Arrive Early:** Plan to arrive 20 minutes early to get settled in and avoid being late. This is a special note to folks (like me!) who think that they can get anywhere in the universe in 10 minutes or less. Arriving late can hurt you. If you're more than 15 minutes late you may forfeit your appointment and be required to pay an additional exam fee.

- **Travel Light:** Leave the big purse and/or bulging briefcase at home or in the car. The test centers often don't have space to securely store large items and you are *not* allowed bring those items into the exam room with you, anyway.

NOTE: You cannot bring your wallet or watch into the exam room with you. You cannot have anything in your pockets including tissues, cell phones, or money of any type. All pocket contents must be removed prior to entering the exam room. Only two items are allowed: you and your ID. The proctor provides scratch paper and pencil.

POINTER: Plan for the Unexpected

"I visited the test center a couple of weeks before my exam. This turned out to be a good thing, because there are various buildings on campus and various entrances for each building. On exam day, I ate a peanut butter sandwich before I left home for brain fuel. I planned to arrive at the testing center 90 minutes early to allow for visiting the restroom, reviewing some note cards, and having a little time to relax. Turns out, I did encounter an accident on my way to the test center, had to take an alternative route, and was delayed 30 minutes. I was very glad I had planned this in advance so I could arrive at the testing center 'centered' instead of 'scattered.'"

~**Renie McClay**, CPLP | Inspired Learning, LLC | www.inspiredtolearn.net

What does success look like?

When you are successful on the CPLP Knowledge Exam, you will receive a **CPLP Score Report** similar to the one below:

ATD Certification Institute (ATD CI)

Certified Professional in Learning and Performance (CPLP)

Score Report

This is to certify that:

Name: Jane Doe

ID #: 222

Examination Date: 03/21/15

Address line 1: 123 Main St

City, State, Zipcode: Chicago, Illinois, 60601

was successful in achieving a passing score on the CPLP Knowledge Exam.

The examination covers the following areas:

Diagnostic Indicators:

–Instructional Design: 84%

–Training Delivery: 83%

–Performance Improvement: 78%

–Evaluating Learning Impact: 71%

–Managing Learning Programs: 83%

–Coaching: 72%

–Integrated Talent Management: 72%

–Change Management: 76%

–Knowledge Management: 71%

These test results were achieved on an examination designed to measure key knowledge as defined by the ATD Certification Institute and based on the latest "ASTD Competency Study: The Training & Development Profession Redefined." Use of these test results for any other purpose is not consistent with the design of the examination.

Submission of a successful Work Product is required before certification will be granted. Complete details on the requirements for the Work Product submission and deadlines can be obtained at: www.td.org/Certification

Please contact certification@td.org if you have a change of address.

Did You Know?

According to ATD CI, the passing rate for the CPLP Knowledge Exam is roughly 75%? That means 1 in 4 candidates fail.

Believe me, in the years I've been coaching people through this certification process, I've never met a CPLP candidate who wants to fail the CPLP Knowledge Exam!

In addition to the emotional impact and disappointment that one often feels after failing the CPLP Knowledge Exam, not passing the CPLP Knowledge Exam also means:

– Trying to figure out what went wrong and how to be successful the second time around

– Paying fees for retesting

– Waiting until the next testing window to open, which could be months away

– More hours, days, weeks—sometimes months!—of additional study preparation

– A delay in achieving your certification

If you do **not** pass the CPLP Knowledge Exam the first time, you are not alone, and you are in good company. It's not uncommon for successful learning professionals to not pass on the first try. Figure out where you struggled, reach out to other candidates, dig in, study, and get ready for the next time. Consider the other study options available that you may not have utilized the first time—perhaps individualized coaching or a more structured study group will help. Whatever you do, take some time to reflect on what may have contributed to these results, develop a plan to overcome these challenges, and begin again.

Master Step Seven Now: Taking the CPLP Knowledge Exam

Before Exam Day

- [ ] If reasonable, practice traveling to the exam center prior to your scheduled exam day

- [ ] Locate the building and if possible, the room

- [ ] Note any construction or potential things to delay your arrival on exam day

- [ ] Practice sitting for 150 minutes

- [ ] Review your notes

Exam Day

- [ ] Eat complex carbohydrates with lean protein to give yourself energy

- [ ] Arrive early to collect yourself

- [ ] Be sure to bring only those things you need:

  - Two forms of ID

Exam Tips

- [ ] Consider how you are going to use Mark for Review

☐ Be sure to take breathing breaks during the exam

☐ Plan for dealing with a question that "throws" you. What will you do?

Tips by Learning/Information Processing Style:

Visual

☐ Try to visualize your study materials. Remember that graphic or colorful note card that explained the concept you are facing.

Auditory

☐ Read the questions aloud, silently to yourself— lip movements help.

Read/Write

☐ Doodle on the scratch paper while you read/respond to questions.

Kinesthetic

☐ Practice "fidgeting" with a pencil prior to Exam Day. Plan for fidgeting with the pencil the proctor gives you as a way to appropriately relieve physical energy while taking the exam.

☐ Doodle on the scratch paper while you read/respond to questions.

Multi-Modal

☐ Think about your study tools and study groups. Do you remember someone saying something about this content? Can you picture the information in your study materials?

TIP: Practice these techniques as you study, so they become a habit by the time you reach exam day!

POINTERS:

Before the Exam—How You Prepare

Mental and physical well-being are important to any exam success. Try to incorporate exercising or, at minimal, stretching into your daily routine. Get the oxygenated blood going to your brain. Practice breathing to help reduce anxiety. Eat breakfast and drink water. And most importantly—get a good night's rest the night before! Put the book down and get some sleep—you'll be better for it!

– Enter the exam in attack mode. Remember, you are there to defeat the exam!

– Don't become quickly discouraged

– Remind yourself that you ARE prepared

– Remind yourself you are a seasoned professional with the required experience

– Remind yourself that this exam doesn't define you—you are no less of a person whatever the outcome

Get up and Stretch!

Our brain needs oxygenated blood. Factor some time into your 150 minutes to get up and stretch. Get that oxygenated blood flowing into the brain."

~**Coline Son Lee**, CPLP | Everest CS

Conclusion:
Putting It All Together

It is a wonderful feeling of personal power and effectiveness after you pass the CPLP Knowledge Exam! Keep these 7 Steps to CPLP Knowledge Exam mastery in mind as you prepare for your Exam Day:

1. Review the CPLP Program Process and Policies

2. Determine Where You Are/Set Your Baseline

3. Identify Your Learning Preferences & Study Style

4. Create Your Study Plan & Assemble Study Materials

5. Study, Practice, and Prepare

6. Conduct a Reality Check

7. Take the CPLP Knowledge Exam

The CPLP Designation

The number of organizations and individuals who recognize the value of the CPLP certification is growing. The CPLP designation following your name signifies your solid foundation of experience in workplace learning and performance and your ability to have a positive impact on bottom-line results.

What's Next?

After you've completed the Knowledge Exam, take a moment to celebrate. Then, collect yourself and get ready to complete some final steps for this phase of the CPLP certification. You'll want to look ahead at some things to help you prepare for the next phase.

Get Organized

Now is a good time to begin organizing your thoughts for the Work Product. Remember your trusty friend and constant resource, Appendix F? Go back to that document and review the sections for the Work Product. Specifically look for the process and criteria for the CPLP Work Product. This will give you a sense of what you need to accomplish.

Think about your current projects. Which projects that you have recently completed, or are currently working on, come to mind when reviewing the

CPLP Work Product submission requirements? Begin narrowing down the list of projects that may be good to showcase.

Review the window for the CPLP Work Product. When do you need to submit your work product documentation? Estimate what portion of the requirements you may have or be able to easily come up with.

Begin to locate resources to help with the Work Product: materials, documentation, people to help answer your questions, review your work and guide you along in this process.

POINTER: Plan Extra Time

"Plan on spending at least 2 to 3 times more time than you think you'll need on the work product. Your inner perfectionist will assert itself.

Allow plenty of time to circulate your work product package to a trusted colleague or two to review. They will helpfully point things out that you will probably want to address."

~**Janet DiVincenzo**, CPLP | University of California, Irvine

After you earn a passing score on the CPLP Knowledge Exam, it is time to finalize your Work Product for submission—the last and final phase of the CPLP certification process.

The Work Product submission portion of the certification process requires that you submit a project you have completed within three (3) years of successful completion of the CPLP Knowledge Exam.

The CPLP Work Product contains specific samples of your work, along with your written responses to ten (10) essay questions about your work—what you did, why you took the approach you did, who you worked with, how you managed the project work, etc.

ATD CI estimates that it takes candidates a minimum of 60 hours to assemble work samples, respond to essay questions, and prepare the submission.

You should also allow additional time to obtain the necessary signatures for the Work Product Release Form, which contains participant release signatures.

Unless you made previous scheduling arrangements, your Work Product is due within 8 to 12 weeks upon successful completion of the CPLP Knowledge Exam, so plan carefully.

Typically, the entire CPLP certification process, from registration to completing the program, takes roughly 6 to 8 months.

At the time of this writing, your Work Product submission must relate to one of four (4) Areas of Expertise:

1. Instructional Design

2. Training Delivery

3. Performance Improvement

4. Managing Learning Programs

All Work Products require documentation of the actual work you did. For example, if Delivering Training is your chosen AOE, you are required to provide a 20-minute recording of your facilitation of a class (see the CPLP Certification Handbook, Part 3 for specific details and requirements).

All CPLP Work Product submissions, regardless of AOE, consist of the following four (4) components:

Project Relationships

You describe and demonstrate how you worked with people—stakeholders and sponsors.

Plans

You describe and demonstrate how you planned your work—from identifying your organization's requirements, to analyzing needs, to determining solutions.

Outputs

You describe and demonstrate how you implemented solutions and managed resources.

Outcomes

You describe and demonstrate how you monitored progress and evaluated results during and after implementation.

An expert review committee evaluates each submission based on specific criteria for each component, relevant to the key actions and essential elements for the submitted AOE. A Scoring Guide for each AOE is included in the CPLP Certification Handbook, Part 3.

Candidates officially become CPLP certified once they receive a passing score on their CPLP Work Product submission.

Checklist: What's Next?

After the CPLP Knowledge Exam

☐ Take a moment to celebrate!

☐ Look at the timeframe for the Work Product

☐ Begin thinking about the project you will showcase in your Work Product (if you haven't already done so)

☐ Review the process and criteria for the CPLP Work Product to have a framework of the next step and its requirements

☐ Locate resources to help with your CPLP Work Product submission, including: example submissions, checklists & job aids, tips & tricks, facilitated online and in-classroom training options.

Review Owl's Ledge CPLP Work Product submission preparation options: http://bit.ly/OWL_CPLPwp

~ Trish Uhl, PMP, CPLP

SPEAKER, TRAINER, SEMINAR LEADER

Trish Uhl is an internationally recognized expert in learning and performance, and a sought-after CPLP and ATD Competency Model speaker, trainer, and author.

Trish, the Owl's Ledge LLC founder and CEO, is passionate about helping people and the organizations they serve to meet the challenges of the Global Knowledge Economy.

Trish's work addresses these challenges from both ends of the spectrum—from consulting with executive leadership on learning strategy, to assisting individuals in aligning to their professional competency models and achieving professional certification.

Trish holds the perspective that competitive advantage and the new value proposition lies in people—human capital—the knowledge, skills, and experiences embodied by the workforce.

Trish firmly believes that meeting the demands of this new era requires development of learning and performance professionals with solid business, collaboration, and communication skills who can develop the 21st century workforce and lead efforts to organizational transformation, globalization, innovation, and strategic enablement.

On a mission to transform learning and performance from reactive and tactical, to strategic and responsive, Trish consults as a Learning Strategist using her experience with global teams, information technology, project management, training, and change management, to assist organizations in aligning their learning-related initiatives to the organization's strategic objectives.

Addressing the need at both ends, Trish also takes a grassroots approach in working with ATD Certified Professional in Learning and Performance (CPLP) candidates to help them adhere to the ATD Competency Model and be successful in the CPLP credentialing program. As a CPLP pilot pioneer herself, being one of the first—worldwide—to achieve the CPLP credential, Trish is dedicated to building the 21st century workforce one CPLP candidate at a time.

Recognized as a leader in the learning and performance industry, Trish is a recipient of Training magazine's Top Young Trainer Award and is a contributing author of two books—10 Steps to Successful Teams (ATD Press) and Fortify Your Sales Force: Leading and Training Exceptional Teams (Pfeiffer)—both available on www.amazon.com.

Trish volunteers globally with the Association for Talent Development (ATD) on a variety of committees and is proud to serve on her local ATD chapter's Board of Directors. Trish served as the 2011 President, Chicagoland ASTD (CCASTD).

In over 20 years of dedication, Trish's ongoing responsibilities continue to include helping organizations and people become ready, willing, and able to manage change and transitions.

Trish's keynote speeches, talks, and seminars are described as "inspiring, entertaining, informative, and motivational." Her audiences include Fortune 500 companies and every size of business and association.

Call for full information on booking Trish to speak at your next meeting or conference.

Some topics include:

　–CPLP Boot Camp

　–Learning Redefined — Gamification

　–Blended Learning

　–Change Practitioner's Toolkit

Trish will carefully customize her talk for you and for your needs.

Visit Owl's Ledge at: www.owls-ledge.com
for more information or call (630) 510-1461 today for a free promotional package.

Join the Owl's Ledge Community

Read our Blog | astdcplp.blogspot.com

Follow me on Twitter | @trishuhl

Follow us on Facebook |
www.facebook.com/OwlsLedge

Connect with me on LinkedIn
| www.linkedin.com/in/trishuhl

Jump in on the Adventure on Pinterest
| http://bit.ly/CPLP_Pinterest

Owl's Ledge Study Materials

Owl's Ledge—the Creators of CPLPCOACH.com—the ONLY Web site dedicated to CPLP Knowledge Exam and CPLP Work Product Workshops and Prep Tools

Visit www.CPLPCOACH.com to access a full set of electronic, mobile, and printable test prep tools to help you thoroughly prepare for the exam. These include:

- Multiple CPLP Practice Tests

- 300+ CPLP Practice Questions

- 500+ Flash Cards (available via smartphone, tablet, online & print)

- Online games and puzzles to practice applying concepts and defining terminology

- Recorded sessions facilitated by CPLP designees and industry leaders

- Accelerated learning tools and techniques to help CPLP candidates retain what they learn and apply it so they improve their exam performance!

Why Owl's Ledge?

– We are the CPLP certification experts! Owl's Ledge CEO and founder, Trish Uhl, launched the CPLP certification prep market in 2005 by designing, developing, & delivering the first CPLP practice exams to CPLP Pilot Pioneers in July 2005.

– Trish and the Owl's Ledge team have helped U.S. and global CPLP candidates to successfully achieve CPLP certification every year in every cohort ever since.

– Owl's Ledge is the official CPLP study prep partner for global organizations—like Hilton Worldwide, Saudi Aramco Oil & Gas, and the PETRONAS Leadership Centre—dedicating resources to helping their candidates to be successful in CPLP certification.

– All Owl's Ledge facilitators are CPLP certified and possess deep knowledge and skills in the areas of expertise they teach.

– Owl's Ledge offers the only available 24/7 self-study and blended learning CPLP prep courses — worldwide!

Owl's Ledge also offers online and in-classroom training for CPLP candidates in the United States and around the world.

Visit the Owl's Ledge web site for details at: www.owls-ledge.com

EXTRAS! Purchase of this book includes access to "extras" — additional tricks, tips, and information to help you prepare for the CPLP Knowledge Exam.

Access this information at
http://bit.ly/CPLP_KEbookextras

Have this book with you when you visit the Web site.

Owl's Ledge — Today

Founded by Trish Uhl in 2003, Owl's Ledge LLC is a learning & performance and project management consulting firm that designs, develops, and delivers business results.

We pride ourselves on taking a holistic approach to developing learning programs that integrate a wide range of disciplines, from business acumen, to change management, to organizational development, to incorporating the best in adult learning theory.

Using this approach, we help learning organizations become transformative, global, innovative, and strategically enabled.

Which supports our mission:

Empowering learning and performance professionals to be ready, willing, and able to address mission critical business needs and face the challenges ahead.

The Owl's Ledge Story

"Owl's Ledge" is an homage to the Uhl family; as the name was originally coined by Trish's mother, Karen, back in the 1970s. It's a play on words—"Uhl" in old German means "wise, old owl."

Karen used the name for her own company, a cattery—yes, cattery—where she bred, raised, and showed Siamese cats. Matter of fact, you can find ads and listings for the original Owl's Ledge in old copies of Cat Fancy and *Cat Fancier* magazines, including one featuring Trish's first cat, Namtaal.

Tom, Trish's father, is the artist who created the familiar owl logo for his wife.

So, in 2003, when Trish was considering names for her new consulting firm, she took inspiration from her mother's battered business card, which she carried in her wallet since her mother passed away from cancer in the late 1970s.

Since then, Owl's Ledge has continued to attract members of the Uhl family, including Trish's brother, Jason. Jason, a teenager at the time, wrote the first Owl's Ledge slogan—"Owl's Ledge: We'll take you from computer stumped to computer savvy!" He's been Trish's Chief Marketing Officer ever since.

Owl's Ledge—The CPLP Certification Experts!

We are the CPLP certification experts—and it shows! Owl's Ledge offers the most effective, innovative CPLP Knowledge Exam & Work Product courses available. Our courses use Accelerated Learning Theory and model Adult Learning Theory to present more content in a shorter period of time and instill more information and practical techniques than other courses. We are also constantly improving our courses based on input from the candidates we work with.

Our courses are developed in accordance with the ATD Competency Model and global learning and performance best practices. Owl's Ledge CPLP prep courses are taught by certified learning and performance professionals (CPLPs) who are experienced learning professionals and highly rated online facilitators.

Owl's Ledge Testimonials

"I am thankful for the Saturday morning classes, as they kept me on track to study each week. I thought the exam was very difficult but am totally relieved to say 'I passed.'"

~Technical Training Specialist, Medical Device Company

"I just wanted to let you know that I PASSED the Knowledge Exam!!! I couldn't believe it... I think that survey at the end of the exam was the longest survey I've ever done. I can't tell you both how much I appreciate your help with preparing for the exam. I was completely anxiety ridden (as you're both aware), and your advice was more than helpful."

~Training & Operations, Major Hotel Chain

"Owl's Ledge was a great resource for helping find out what I needed to prepare."

~Curriculum Development Specialist, National Insurance Company

"The support and information I got from Owl's Ledge was invaluable."

~Curriculum Designer, Major Retail Store

"Trish is my colleague, my mentor, and most importantly, my friend. Trish's experience and leadership capabilities are second to none. I've benefited from all of this with our continued work on the ASTD CPLP certification and re-certification process."

~Training & Development Manager, National Eldercare Provider

Acknowledgements

The words and experiences in this book were not possible without the support and encouragement from a whole host of people who challenged me to exceed my limits, push my boundaries, and refine my craft.

To them—the many people who were an intricate part of authoring this book—I say: Thank you!

Thank you very much to my original writing and editing team, Renie McClay, Louann Swedberg, and Kit Libenschek who always know how to bring out the best in my words and for seeing my potential in making this book a reality – especially when I couldn't.

YOU ROCK!

A hearty SHOUT OUT of heartfelt thanks to Michael Courter and Alex Courter – the father & son follow-up writing and editing team who have HUSTLED to help me get subsequent releases out as the CPLP program continues to evolve and the American Society for Training & Development (ASTD) re-brands to the Association for Talent Development (ATD).

I'M HERE!

And I'm GLAD you both are HERE too! :-D

Special thanks to M.E. Majeske for her cheerleading, coaching, love, and support.

To Lou Russell, at times partner-in-crime and other times, patron saint—and at all times a FABULOUS role model and great friend. TAH-DAH!

Sincere gratitude to fellow CPLPs Leonard Cochran, Larry Straining, Diane Smith, Coline Son Lee, and Marilyn Zwissler for their sharp editing skills.

A SHOUT OUT to the first Owl's Ledge "minion"— Katelind Karol Hays—for her assistance and steady sense of humor. I can't tell you how glad I am that you jumped in!

Thank you to CPLP Fellows and mentors, Elaine Biech and Bob Pike, for their guidance, counsel, coaching, and encouragement.

A word of thanks to Kimo Kippen for his leadership and willingness to listen; I aspire to one day emulate his grace and diplomacy.

To the generous contributors to this book—Lisa Haneberg, Sharon Wingron, Jim "Mr. Energy" Smith, Jr., Maureen Orey, Ken Phillips, Lou Russell, Jim & Wendy Kirkpatrick, Gerald Haman, Bob Pike—for sharing your work so we can create a world that works better!

To all of the CPLP designee and candidate colleagues around the globe who lit the path so that others may follow. I am so very proud that this book contains so many of your comments, tips, and personal experiences!

To Ike and Sarah Gilbert many thanks for taking the iBook adventure with me. May we always have cheese. You know, regular cheese. From the Steve.

To my friends and family, Sandy Reeser, Putnam Texel, Larry & Dixie Haltom, Jason, Jenny, & Lily Uhl who fed me—heart, soul, & spirit—along the way.

All of you deserve much more than the simple thank you that appears here.

Thank you for helping me write "Mastering the CPLP."

It's finally done!

Again! :-)

YAY CAKE!

30 March, 2015

(v2 Updates completed from the comfort of my home in the wilds of the Chicago suburbs - USA)

And More Praise

"No one knows CPLP prep like Trish, and it shows in this book. Her years of experience supporting learning professionals in preparing for certification come through on each page, and it is certainly a MUST READ for anyone who is considering their CPLP certification. In classic Trish style, this book starts and ends with the learner. She really focuses on empowering professionals to be effective learners in this exciting phase of their career development."

~**RICHARD H. SITES**, Ed. D., Vice President, Client Services, Allen Interactions Inc. Co-Author of *Leaving ADDIE for SAM*

"Trish Uhl has done it again! She always shares tips, tools, and life lessons with her friends, colleagues, and clients! Now she has provided a GPS for *YOU* to prepare for and pass the CPLP exam. Trish Uhl is on *FIIIRRREEEE*! She has a keen knack for helping people get 'it,' whatever their 'it' is. This time, the 'it' is the CPLP Knowledge Exam. After you devour this reader-friendly instruction manual, filled with Trish's greatest hits, you WILL ace this test! No excuses! Trish, here's a high five! You just get better and better!"

~**JIM "MR. ENERGY" SMITH, JR.**, JIMPACT Enterprises, Author of *The No Excuse Guide to Success: No Matter What Your Boss — or Life — Throws at You*

"Are you thinking about pursing the ASTD CPLP certification? Read this book before you begin and read it again, during your journey, to guide you along the way. Trish Uhl answers hundreds of questions that anyone considering, and pursing, the CPLP certification would want to know. She also shares her insights from helping hundreds of candidates become certified. Many helpful tips from other CPLPs and CPLP candidates are included. No doubt, you will find this book to be invaluable to you."

~**LEONARD COCHRAN**, CPLP, Manager, Learning Programs, Commercial College, Hilton Worldwide University

"Trish's advice and support team for preparing for the CPLP exam and Work Product sets the standard for coaching services for ANY certification."

~**JASON DE LUCA**, Managing Director Smart Partners KK, Tokyo Japan

"Trish Uhl provides a primer that is direct, honest, and accurate. Too many CPLP candidates underestimate the rigor of the process and are disappointed with their results. Read this book, then follow the Owl's Ledge approach, and you'll significantly increase your odds of passing the CPLP Knowledge Exam."

~**SHARON WINGRON**, CPLP, President, Wings of Success LLC

"Amazing... just amazing. Trish has taken all the guesswork out, which allows the person pursuing the certification to focus on their preparation, and not all the administrative distractors around how to get started. She has done the field of L&D a tremendous service. If the Chicago Cubs had Trish on their team, they'd have broken their 108-year drought. This is World Series stuff!"

~**TERRENCE DONAHUE**, Global Training Director, Emerson

"Trish Uhl has written a practical, appealing, and truly examination-oriented study guide to help learning and performance professionals effectively prepare for and pass the CPLP Knowledge Exam. This book not only gives the right strategy and proven approaches for study, but also mentally steers you towards success. Trish has used concise and conversational style to engage readers to be intellectually, emotionally, and mentally prepared for the Exam. I highly recommend this as a must-read book for anyone pursuing the CPLP certification!"

~**PETER YIP,** President, ASTD Global Network Hong Kong

"Read this book, and take all you see to heart. Contained in these pages are hundreds of lessons learned, some undoubtedly painfully gained. And here they are, for the benefit of all. As Trish so often likes to say, no one becomes a CPLP on their own. If you are anything like I was at the beginning of this process, you've decided you want this designation, but you may be stumped where to begin. I can attest from personal experience: Start here."

~**CORY M. ARCHIBALD**, CPLP, Tarlac, Philippines

"Having recently earned my CPLP and fresh from the trenches, I know that this book will prepare you for the journey! I was overwhelmed at first and not sure where to start. Trish Uhl gives you all the information you need to know and directs you to many resources. Owl's Ledge showed me how to develop a study plan that worked perfectly for me. Additionally, the Owl's Ledge Knowledge Exam Prep course helped me stay on track. Success! "

~**JANN IACO**, CPLP, eLearning and Training Specialist, Global Home Furnishings Retailer

"If only I had Trish's powerful book, I would not have flunked the CPLP Knowledge Exam."

~**SIVASAILAM THIAGARAJAN (THIAGI)**, Author of *Jolts! Activities to Wake Up and Engage Your Participants*

"With 7 key steps, a dose of experienced-based reality, along with insight and tips from successful CPLP recipients, Trish Uhl pulls back the curtain on the mysteries behind passing the CPLP exam. Every WLP professional serious about earning their CPLP certification needs this book! What a confidence builder!"

~**WALT HANSMANN,** CPLP, Manager of Instructional Design, McJunkin Red Man Corporation (MRC)

"Trish has assembled the most helpful elements possible to get ready for the CPLP exam. They're realistic, promising, and encouraging for the candidates to put together a checklist of everything needed to not just pass the exam—they can also bolster and expand the toolkits for today's WLP professionals. Whether you are sticking your toe in the water, or signed up for the next exam window, this book will help you put your personal study plan together and help you boost your knowledge levels in ways you never thought possible."

~**JASON GARDNER**, CPLP, Las Vegas, Nevada

"This book lays out the steps for a successful CPLP Knowledge Exam which Trish enhances by including checklists for you to personalize. In addition, each step, each section is full of tips and testimonials from other professionals who have already gone through the process and were successful on the CPLP Knowledge Exam. Mastering the CPLP: How to Successfully Prepare for—and Pass!—the CPLP Knowledge Exam is a great resource for people who are considering sitting for the CPLP Knowledge Exam and is a MUST HAVE for those who are candidates."

~**LARRY STRAINING**, CPLP, Larry's Training, LLC

"This book is the best guide you will find for understanding the CPLP process and preparing for the exam. Trish has gathered recommendations and insights from successful CPLP candidates and shares them with you in a cogent and personal way. You will benefit from their experiences. No matter how you learn, you will find the right mix of study materials, methodologies, and strategies for you."

~MARILYN ZWISSLER, CPLP, Learning Management, Global Process Transformation Project, Rockwell Automation

"Trish's book offers you a robust roadmap on how you should plan, study, practice and prepare to succeed on the CPLP Knowledge Exam. In addition, Trish guides you to discover your own learning preference and study style, as well as discusses the importance of emotional intelligence and overall well-being during this journey. Furthermore, this book provides a variety of additional tips and application-proven strategies used by successful CPLP candidates that you can put to use immediately."

~TATIANY MARANHÃO MELECCHI, MM, CPLP, Saint Louis, Vice President of Saint Louis ASTD Chapter

"I wish this resource was available when I was going through the rigorous CPLP experience. I point peers considering CPLP to the resources provided by Trish and Owl's Ledge. This book provides great tips and serves as an excellent guide to anyone considering the CPLP."

~DAVID KELLY, CPLP, CRP, Program Director, The eLearning Guild

Made in the USA
Lexington, KY
31 August 2015